The Home Decorator's Tile Sourcebook

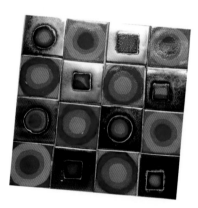

The Home Decorator's Tile Sourcebook

A Complete Guide to Tiling in the Home

Morwenna Brett

APPLE

A QUARTO BOOK

Copyright © 2008 Quarto Inc.

Published in 2008 by
Apple Press
7 Greenland Street
London NW1 0ND

www.apple-press.com

ISBN: 978-1-84543-228-7

Conceived, designed and produced by
Quarto Publishing plc
The Old Brewery
6 Blundell Street
London
N7 9BH

QUAR.TBI

Project editor: Katie Hallam
Copy editor: Trisha Telep
Art director: Caroline Guest
Art editor: Natasha Montgomery
Designer: Paul Griffin
Illustrator: Kong Kang Chen
Picture researchers: Claudia Tate, Gwen Campbell,
Kay Rowley

Creative director: Moira Clinch
Publisher: Paul Carslake

Manufactured by Modern Age Repro House Ltd.,
Hong Kong
Printed in China by Midas Printing International Ltd.

9 8 7 6 5 4 3 2 1

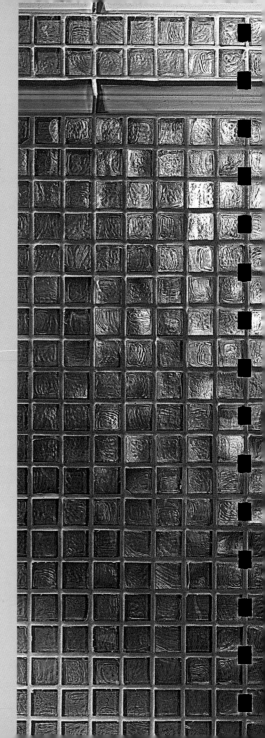

contents

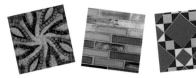

Introduction 6

About this Book 7

Designing with Tiles 8

Living with Tiles 18

Types of Tile 26

Ceramic 28

Terracotta and Saltillo 32

Porcelain 34

Stone 36

Glass 42

Metallics 44

Mosaic and Picture Tiles 46

Antique 48

Cork and Leather 50

Linoleum, Vinyl, Rubber 52

Tile Directory 54

Red 56

Orange 80

Yellow 94

Green 110

Blue 134

Neutrals 158

Black and White 178

Metallics 194

The Techniques 206

Adhesives and Grout 208

Tools 210

Ordering 212

Walls 213

Floors 232

Resources and Suppliers 250

Index 254

Credits 256

introduction

The only tiles I really remember from my childhood are the industrial cream and brown ones that lined the town's swimming pool, and the occasional dingy tiles from a floral panel in a fire surround. Both of these types of tiling were then considered old-fashioned in an era addicted to tearing out original features and painting everything white.

I didn't realize that tiles could be more than just functional until a student backpacking trip around the Middle East much later. The mosque cities of Iran showed me what an artist can do with tiles: taking simple shapes of clay, decorating them with dazzling blues, turquoises and reds, and creating domes and façades that take your breath away with their elegance and beauty.

Today, tiles are enjoying a renaissance. Tile-makers all over the world are combining new techniques with old skills to reinvent the tile for the modern home. No longer just a utilitarian surface, tiles can once again make a design statement in their own right, with luminous glass, glittering mosaics and delicious glazes set off by elegant stones and floor slates.

Once you start looking, the choice is dazzling. You can create any look you want. Tough, beautiful and infinitely varied, tiles are essential for modern living.

Monica Bett

To my father, who showed me how to write professionally.

about this book

A well-tiled floor or wall will give you immense pleasure for a long time, keeping its looks for much longer than a carpet or wallpaper that has to be renewed after only a few years of life. This book is a guide to choosing and using tiles successfully, so that you can take pride in the finished result, knowing you have created something that will last and look good for many years to come.

Tile directory

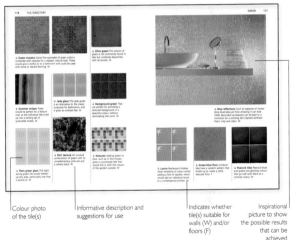

Designing with tiles
pages 8–17
Designer tips on working with tiles, the results it's possible to achieve, and getting your own project under way.

Living with tiles
pages 18–25
A room-by-room look at how to make the best of tiles all around the home.

Types of tile
pages 26–53
Tiles in detail – the pros and cons of the different types, from hard tiling to resilient floor tiles.

Tile directory
pages 54–205
Your indispensable guide to the array of tiles available. Grouped by colour for ease of reference, with useful styling and colour scheming advice.

Colour photo of the tile(s) | Informative description and suggestions for use | Indicates whether tile(s) suitable for walls (W) and/or floors (F) | Inspirational picture to show the possible results that can be achieved

The techniques
pages 206–249
Finally, there's guidance on planning, cutting and fitting your tiles – essential information to make your project run smoothly, both before and after you make your purchase.

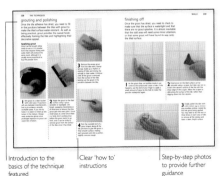

The techniques

Introduction to the basics of the technique featured | Clear 'how to' instructions | Step-by-step photos to provide further guidance

designing with tiles

Tiles are a decorator's dream material. Immensely practical and adaptable, they can be used for almost any surface. There's a tile for every room and every space – from porcelain, terracotta, glass, metal and mosaic, to the softer finishes of leather, vinyl, linoleum and rubber.

Most tiles are extremely hard-wearing, and many of them take water in their stride. Excellent for surfaces that are subject to moisture, they are also easy to clean and keep hygienic, which means they are favourites for bathrooms, kitchens and utility rooms. However, their cool, hard finish is extremely appealing in other rooms, particularly in hotter climates.

Tiles can easily be made the key point of a design scheme. A simple tiled floor, for example, gives an instant sense of timeless antiquity. Because people have been designing with tiles for hundreds of years, tiles are part of a wide variety of traditional styles, which can be recreated effortlessly using either antique tiles or modern reproductions. Modern designers have given us new surfaces and finishes to play with, from the new brilliantly hard-wearing porcelain tiles to glamorous metallics and glass mosaics.

Simple to use, tiles can cover large areas easily, and the subtle texture of their repeating shapes means that even an area of single colour never looks boring. There is scope, however, for huge creativity. By using borders, colour contrasts, size and texture, you can create a unique scheme for every room.

The green home

Tiles have health and environmental advantages as well, and they are a good choice for use in a home with an allergy sufferer. Carpets and natural floorings such as jute and seagrass – however well you clean them – will always be a source of dust and dirt. Tiled floors are more straightforward: they form an allergen-free surface that is easy to keep clean and doesn't harbour dust mites. Most tiles are made of natural products and are extremely hardy. Their life cycle, therefore, including final disposal, is more environmentally friendly than that of many other decorating products.

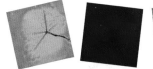

patterns with tiles

Tiles give the designer a huge advantage. Using their simple, repetitive nature to build up a unique design is easy, satisfying and time tested.

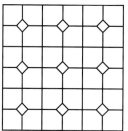

Squares with inserts

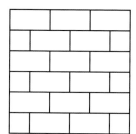

Brick-bond

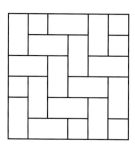

Herringbone

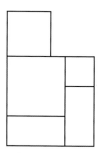

Tile pavement (or *Opus Romana*)

Classic floor tile layouts

Depending on your choice of tile, these four patterns can appear traditional or modern, as you prefer. Lay out a trial area before you start fixing any pattern, to check the joint sizes that will be needed and what grout widths would look best.

Design tips

> Because most tiles are a uniform shape (square or rectangular), there are endless design possibilities for using simple colours before tackling patterned or more complicated tiles.

> In general, keep it simple. Using one colour produces a highly successful and pleasing floor or wall. However, you can combine just a few contrasting colours and sizes to make an extremely effective pattern, such as a chequered floor.

> Border tiles can be used across the top of an area of plain tiles to outline a mirror or to break up a large surface.

> Keep in scale – generally, large tiles are best for large rooms, small ones for smaller places.

> Large-format tiles help break up large areas in a subtle way to create a more intimate space.

> Rules can be broken! A sequence of large-format tiles looks less busy because there are fewer grout lines to break up the surface. Large tiles can often bring simplicity to a small bathroom. However, if you have a lot of complex

surfaces (like a large number of window surrounds), then small tiles (2.5 cm square, for example) make for a neater finish.

> Rectangular tiles can be used to give the illusion of width or height, depending on which way you place them (the eye will follow the longest dimension of the tile).

> Scattered motif tiles don't always look as good as you might think. Keep them grouped together, or put them within a border.

> Picture tiles, mosaics or sets of tiles that form a complete picture or panel look good in outdoor settings, and they can enliven a dreary entrance hall.

> A complex tile pattern needs to be surrounded by simple furnishings, otherwise the room will look too busy.

> Light shades make a room seem larger; dark, rich tones create a more intimate, enclosed environment.

> Rough surfaces create a rustic mood; glossy, shiny surfaces look more urban and sophisticated.

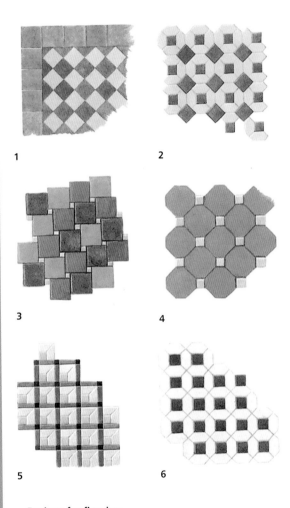

1 2 3 4 5 6

Designs for flooring

The regular, repeating module format of tiles means that designing an individual flooring pattern is easy, if you take some time and experiment with different layouts. Above are a few possibilities based on simple squares and hexagons. Tiles can be combined with a basic border for definition (1), or a hexagon or square can be combined with a small key square as an inset (2,3,4 and 6). The use of contrasting colours in a lattice (5) creates a surprising three-dimensional impression, which can look dramatic but must be used with care, as the optical illusion may be visually unbalancing in some rooms.

Popular tile patterns

The following tile patterns are found in many homes and have widely recognized names:

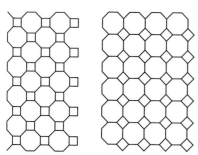

Octagon with square   Octagon with dot

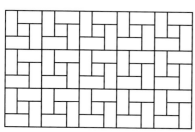

Pinwheel

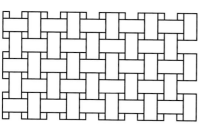

Basket weave

Running board

Which tile flooring?

Tiled flooring falls into two categories:

Hard tile floors

> Metal, marble, granite, glass, ceramic and terracotta.

> Often most expensive form of flooring, very durable but can be cold.

> More difficult to install than other floors, so use a professional unless you are a skilled home renovator.

> Need a strong, inflexible subfloor (the floor surface you plan to fix the tiles to).

Resilient tile floors

> Cork, leather, linoleum, vinyl and rubber.

> Softer underfoot, they feel warmer than hard tiles.

> They are easy to install and clean (except for leather).

> Vinyl, cork and linoleum are inexpensive; rubber costs slightly more; leather is very expensive.

> Because they are the thinnest form of tiles, they need a subfloor that is especially level. It can be more flexible than for hard tile flooring, however.

inspiration

Many larger suppliers have showrooms with displays of stones and tiles put together by designers to give you inspiration. Many tile showrooms also offer an individual design service using computer-aided design (CAD), and they will produce a printout of your chosen design to scale, together with the quantities of tiles needed.

Choosing your tile

Tiles can be used in every room of the home. The principle you must bear in mind is that not all tiles can be used everywhere. What is suitable for a wall may not be appropriate for a floor, for example, and you need to seek advice to make effective design decisions.

For a satisfying result, take your time over your purchase. It's worth borrowing or even buying one or two examples of a tile, taking them home and looking at them in the intended room. The colours of your furnishings, as well as how the room is lit at various times of day, will have an influence on whether the tile is suitable. Once you get them home, tiles will often look different from the way they did in the showroom. They will also look different if placed vertically on a wall, compared to horizontally on a work surface or floor.

▲ **On display** Tile showrooms will often have display areas where you can see how a multicoloured tile will look when it covers a whole wall.

◀ **Be prepared** Tiles should always be set against colour swatches of your paint and fabric – take samples on your searches rather than try to rely on your memory, which may not be as accurate as you think.

Choosing tiles checklist

Are the tiles suitable for the surface?

> Floor tiles are designed to be strong and endure the wear and tear of people walking on them. As you might expect, floor tiles are thicker than other tiles and will withstand heavier loads.

> Wall tiles are usually not strong enough to be walked on. Although you can often use a floor tile on a wall, the opposite doesn't apply.

> Floor tiles can be used on walls, but because they are much harder than wall tiles, problems may arise when drilling through them or cutting them to fit around pipework, basins or windows.

> Bathroom floor tiles and tiles used in wet areas such as swimming pools and shower stalls need to be non-slip. The wrong choice of tile would be very dangerous here. You need either a rough, less-polished surface, or a small format like mosaic where the grout lines and edges give grip.

> If you live in an area of the world with frost conditions, outdoor tiles must be non-absorbent, so they don't take in water, which can expand and damage the tile when it freezes. Conservatories also need tiles that can withstand freezing and thawing. This type of tile is called vitreous or impervious: porcelain is a good example, along with some stones and slates.

Can the subfloor take the weight?

> One vital factor in the choice of tiled flooring is whether or not the subfloor can support the weight.

> Concrete ground-level floors can usually support any hard tile floor, and suspended concrete flooring in modern blocks of flats should also be able to bear a heavy flooring material. If you are in any doubt, consult a builder or a structural engineer before going ahead. Be very cautious when putting heavy tiles on a wooden subfloor, especially if you intend to use a mortar bed. Professional advice is essential here.

▶ **Choose wisely** Patterns like this can be achieved with all sorts of tile, from marble and stone to lighter vinyl and linoleum; just make sure you choose the right tiling for the strength of the subfloor.

finishes

Tiles come in a multitude of finishes, from rough and matt, to highly glazed and shiny. You need to make sure that the finish of your tile is suitable for where you want to use it.

Some tiles may need sealing once they have been laid. Make sure you see a sealed sample before purchase because the sealant usually enhances the natural colours and textures of the tile, in the same way varnish does for wood grain, influencing the finished effect.

Edges

Generally, tiles have a gently rounded edge, so there is a small gap between each one when they are laid out. This gap gets filled with grout, a plaster-like material that completes the whole installation. Tiles that are cut with modern laser cutters, however, have rectified edges and very narrow grout lines.

Rustic tiles (such as Saltillo tiles) have very rough edges and have to be laid with a generous space between them, which is then filled by the grout. This wide grout line can have quite an impact on the overall effect of the design, so try to see them installed at a showroom to check whether or not you like the look.

▲ **Mix and match** A mixed assortment of tiles can be used together, if you apply a little imagination and creativity. This is a casual, informal effect that would work well for a country porch or veranda.

budget

Least expensive – standard-format ceramic
More expensive – porcelain, large format, mosaic, handmade
Most expensive – natural stone

Tiles vary hugely in price. You will probably have to pay more for a tile that also has coordinating trim options available (such as borders and edgings), in addition to the basic field tile, but this may be worth it in order to create a really stylish finish to your project.

More expensive tiles have usually been more time-consuming to produce, involving hand finishing, rich quality glazes and unusual colours.

The cost of your tiles must be balanced with the cost of installation, including the price of the subfloor, grouts, and sealing and cleaning materials. With stone flooring in particular there can be a high added cost for professional fixing and sealing.

Changing floor levels?

The combination of laying a new subfloor plus the added height of the tiles can raise the new floor surface considerably, causing problems with doors, fitted furniture and thresholds from one room to another. Check and plan for this at the design stage.

Do you want under-floor heating?

Almost all forms of tiles will take under-floor heating, but there are different types for different purposes, depending on tile thickness. This needs to be planned from the outset. You will also need to have a suitable power supply in the room for electric under-floor heating. For wet systems, pipework will have to be run as part of the subfloor before the tiles are laid.

LARGE VS SMALL
Large-format tiles require a flatter surface than small-format tiles (which are better at following any slight variations in level). The larger the format the higher the price (particularly with stones), because a larger tile is harder to cut and source.

planning your design

Tile sizes vary from tiny mosaic tiles at 1 cm
(⅓ inch) square, to large floor tiles that can be
60 x 80 cm (24½ x 31½ inches) or even larger. In
particular, if you're using these large tiles, you need
to draw the tile pattern to scale, so that you know
how the tiles are going to lie and be cut. A scale
drawing will show you exactly how many tiles
you are going to use, and it will help your tiler
understand how you want the tiles laid out.

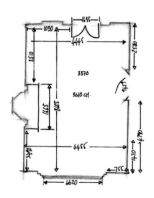

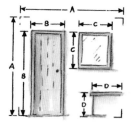

Elevation
An elevation is a scale drawing of a wall, similar
to the floor plan (top right), that allows you to
calculate the number of tiles you might need.
You can make allowances for doors, windows and
other architectural features in your calculations,
but remember to allow for wastage too.

Scale plan
A scale plan can help you figure out a floor tile
pattern. Take several photocopies of it to use
for rough initial planning; you can then trace
your design onto plain tracing paper and use
coloured pencils or pens to try out different colour
combinations. You can also use the tracing to help
you position a central motif or border effectively.
Once you are happy with your design, you can use
the scale drawing to calculate the exact quantities
of each tile required.

◄ **Matching up** Plain tiles or
tiles that can be turned around
without causing problems with
the pattern are the most
economical. The tiles shown
here would be more wasteful,
as the pattern needs to be
carefully matched.

WASTAGE
Using large tiles can be
more wasteful than using
small ones, particularly in a
small area, as there has to
be more cutting to size. In
these circumstances, it is
advisable to allow even
more than the customary
10% extra cost for wastage.

borders and tile mixes

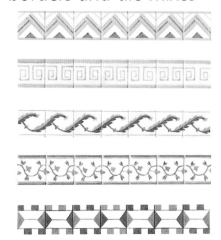

Borders can be either strongly geometric or have more flowing floral elements.

▲ **Size variation** Combining tiles in the same colour but different sizes gives very satisfying results.

▲ **Random effect** Distributing coloured and patterned tiles randomly over an area can be just as pleasing as a regular pattern.

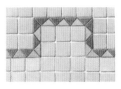

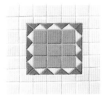

◀ **Border uses** Borders can neaten the edge of a tile area, create a frame or can be used twice for a stronger double border.

living with tiles

The versatility of tiles means they can be used in almost every room in the home. Their hard-wearing, easy-care qualities make them suitable not only for kitchens and bathrooms but also for living rooms and hallways. Tiles have always been used outdoors too, making an attractive transition between the home and the garden, as well as being highly suitable for conservatories and porches.

Small-format mosaics are very versatile for bathrooms, where they can cover large surfaces and the edges of shelves.

◀ **Attention to detail**
Notice how the top of the tile line has been carefully aligned with the bar of the window frame for a clean, professional finish.

kitchens and dining rooms

A kitchen is often the most hardworking area of the home and needs impervious, hygienic and easy-clean surfaces. Tiles perform effortlessly in the kitchen and have been considered the perfect solution for over one hundred years.

Dining rooms need to have an aura of warmth. Use appetite-inducing colours from the warm side of the spectrum, like reds, yellows, oranges or warm neutrals in terracotta. A cool stone or marble tile can look too formal and icy in the dining room unless you live in a climate that is warm all year.

Tiles look great combined with wood tones in both kitchens and dining rooms. From the rich, dark colours of antique oak and rustic country furniture to the blond tones of Scandinavian timber, tiles are a perfect match.

GET THE STYLE

COUNTRY KITCHEN: Use rough slate; encaustic tiles; antique stone; delft tiles; hand-painted floral tiles, scenes and borders; or craft and handmade tiles.

MEDITERRANEAN KITCHEN: Use terracotta; porcelain or ceramic imitations of terracotta; Saltillo; bright glazed tiles in red, blue and sunshine yellow; hand-painted Spanish or Mexican tiles; blue-and-white Portuguese tiles; or hand-painted designs with olives or grapes.

CONTEMPORARY CHIC: Use rubber or linoleum tiles in bright colours, large-format porcelain tiles, glass, metallic tiles, rectangular tiling, polished stones, or neutral black, grey or white set off with slate blue, cream or grey-greens.

◀ **Contrasting texture**
This tiled area emphasizes the contrast between the plain satin finish of the stainless steel and the dimensional glossy cream tiling.

▲ **A touch of class** This unusual mosaic format makes a pleasing, contemporary pattern over the whole wall surface.

◀ **Classic comfort** Traditional tiles in country colours always make for a welcoming kitchen.

Tiling kitchens

> Kitchen surfaces need to stand up to hot pots and pans and food splashes, which make tiles a perfectly functional yet beautiful solution for walls, floors and countertops.

> Use tiles behind cooking, sink and food preparation areas. A splashback behind the stove can be a perfect place to show off a tile mural, picture tiles or a panel of special tiles that are too expensive to use over a larger area.

> Use an epoxy grout (see page 209) on surfaces such as kitchen countertops, where hygiene is an important issue, rather than a conventional water-based grout that will absorb stains and liquids.

> Surfaces in kitchens are often broken up, so don't use complicated designs. Keep it simple and stick to a few main colours unless you have a big area to tile.

> Floors can be made of slate, stone, quarry, ceramic or porcelain tiles, which are easy to care for if properly sealed and will last a very long time.

> Remember, however, that hard tiles are very unforgiving to dropped plates and glasses.

> Linoleum and vinyl floors are easier and cheaper to update than hard flooring.

> Consider a range of tiles that includes matching tile-edging strips for a classy finish to countertops and window surrounds.

bathrooms

Bathrooms used to be cold, functional places, but we are more demanding now and expect them to be luxurious spaces to unwind in, and rooms where we can linger with pleasure. This is where the new affordable mosaics and marbles, or ceramic imitations of marbles, come into the picture. They give any bathroom an instant feeling of effortless luxury. However, one of the most elegant and striking bathroom schemes still remains the simple all-white or all-neutral design, with some geometric tiles or mosaics as contrast. Contrast the simplicity and gloss of these classic tiles with big fluffy towels and you have the perfect area for relaxing.

GET THE STYLE

VICTORIAN HIGH STYLE: Use high-gloss glazed ceramic tiles; tile borders; dados and moulded tiles; greens, creams and reds; black and white chequered flooring; floral designs or tile panels.

CONTEMPORARY CHIC: Use subway tiles, glass, mosaic and ceramic against chrome and stainless steel, refreshing blues and turquoise, tumbled stone and marble, and simple lines. Create a wetroom with all-tile surfaces.

FIVE-STAR HOTEL: Use neutral colours; large-format tiles in stone, travertine, marble or ceramic imitations; tiling over all floor and wall surfaces; clean simple lines; and lighting that is flush with tiled surfaces. Use only one or two different tile styles or sizes throughout.

◀ **Bathroom chic** A simple use of a panel of mosaic within large-format stone or porcelain tiling frames the showerhead and controls.

▼ **High style** If you want to recreate a flamboyant period style, tiles are the perfect way to do it.

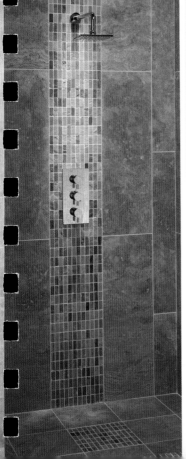

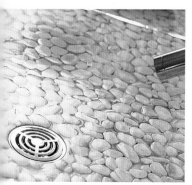

◀ Careful planning
Wetrooms need to be well planned and well built to look good and function properly.

ALL-OVER TILING

Wetrooms give a streamlined, elegant look to any bathroom. They're not just a fashion statement though – level access makes showering safer for children and people with limited mobility.

However, a fully tiled shower is a challenge to any contractor, and any short cuts in the construction will lead to trouble later on. Tile and grout joints can't be relied on to be totally waterproof: water penetrates and collects in floor and wall structures, causing mould and leaks. A shower with a tiled floor needs a waterproofing system beneath the tiles, particularly as modern showers blast the walls with greater pressure than ever before, putting the tiled surface under considerable strain. Fitting waterproof membranes beneath the tiling is essential. Some of these membranes are sheet based, while others are a liquid compound. They aim to resist the normal movement of the room and not become brittle with age.

An additional problem is how to create a slope in the floor to allow the water to run away, leaving a space within it for the drain system itself. Various manufacturers produce prefabricated systems that can be fitted under the tiling, which are lighter than a base constructed out of mortar.

In the end, it all depends on the quality of the workmanship. Use a contractor experienced in the construction of showers and who understands the techniques and the pitfalls.

Tiling bathrooms

> Bathroom floors must be non-slip and able to cope with water. Some tiles become especially slippery when wet. There are many tiles that are perfect for bathroom flooring, but just remember to make sure they are specifically non-slip.

> Bathrooms are usually small, so the price of all the tiles needed will be minimal. This is one room where some extravagant tiles could be affordable to even the most restrictive budgets.

> Due to its small size, the bathroom needs careful planning in order not to look cluttered.

> Too many patterned tiles can be overpowering in a little space.

> Use smaller-format tiles if large tiles would have to be considerably cut up to cope with all the changes of surface. Small mosaics often look good and are an excellent choice for bathrooms.

> Take a sample of your tile home to match to your sink, bath and toilet. Not all whites and creams are the same – a very white bath may make an off-white tile look an unappealing grey.

> Generally, floors get thinner as you move into the upper storeys of a house. Heavy tiles may not be suitable for suspended wood subfloors in a third-floor bathroom.

halls and entranceways

The hallway is a transition area – an opportunity to make a bold and stylish first impression – but it also needs to be welcoming.

▲ **Change of pace** A change in the pattern in this black and white flooring marks a transition area from one part of the hall to another.

▶ **Hard-wearing** Take tiling in narrow hallways up the wall as well as on the floor for a tough approach to daily traffic.

Tiling halls

> Mosaic or multicoloured geometric tiling can be very effective in the hallway, as they might be overpowering if used in a larger space.

> Entrances take a lot of punishment from shoes, strollers, dirty bicycles, wet luggage and shopping. Stone, slate and terracotta are excellent choices for this reason.

> Hallways provide an excellent opportunity to use border tiles or create a geometric pattern, because there's generally less furniture to cover up an elaborate design.

> Victorian wall tiles and panels create interest while still being hard wearing. They are particularly good for very narrow hallways where they can be used up to dado level.

> In warmer climates, you can continue the tiling all the way up the stairway. Patterned tiles on the risers look great, but make sure that your staircase is strong enough to take the extra weight.

> Red, peach, pumpkin, terracotta, apricot and gold are all good colours for entrances.

living rooms

Tiling living rooms

> Make sure the subfloor can take the weight of your choice of tile.

> Hard tiling in the living room needs rugs or carpet squares to add warmth and keep it from seeming harsh and clinical.

> Large-format tiles look good in larger rooms; smaller quarry tiles are perfect in smaller rooms, particularly if you want an informal, cottage style.

> Under-floor heating is a good option to consider if the room is used all day by the family.

GET THE STYLE

CLASSIC ELEGANCE: Use black and white squares; limestone; marble; marble or ceramic tiles with chipped or aged edges; distressed travertine or limestone; small metallic, encaustic or ceramic insert tiles in stone or ceramic flooring.

HIGH VICTORIAN STYLE: Use encaustic tiling; colourful geometric designs; tiles up to dado level with panels; mouldings; arts and crafts, art nouveau or William de Morgan tiles and tube-lined tiles.

MODERN SIMPLICITY: Use large-format ceramic, stone or slate flooring.

COUNTRY WELCOME: Use slate, warm stone, quarry tiles or a tile pattern in terracotta with inserts for the floor.

▲ **Get cosy**
Warm tile colours work very well to keep a living room feeling homely.

▼ **A touch of glamour** The dramatic darkness of these tiles, coupled with soft lighting, gives the area a glamorous ambience.

outdoors

Many homes have a conservatory, porch or veranda that is an attractive transition between the inside and outside. Tiled flooring is an obvious choice to handle the impact of both inside and outside living. Terraces, patios and swimming pools are also highly suited to tiling.

◀ **Living in harmony**
For a simple, harmonious conservatory scheme, match the floor tiles to similar colours in the paintwork and planters.

POOLS

You'll use a specialist team of professionals to install a pool, but the choice of tiles is up to you. And there's no need to go for a complex and expensive pool shape when there are masses of original and striking pool tiles available that will give your pool the "wow" factor all on their own.

> It's very important to choose suitable tiles that are non-slip when wet. Have them installed properly with the recommended adhesives and grouts.

> Although they all look very different, most pool tiles are glazed porcelain and hence they are waterproof and frost proof.

> Cobalt blues and turquoises are always a perfect, classic choice for pool tiles. They give a cooling effect on the hottest day and complement the pale blue of the pool water.

> Pictorial tiles or mosaics really come into their own when used for a pool, either as part of the pool structure or on the surrounding walls. You can buy ready-made pictorial or mosaic panels or have a custom design made. Mosaics are mounted on mesh for ease of installation and just need grouting.

Tiling outdoor areas

> Your flooring needs to be impervious to damp and easy to clean if there are plants in the space.

> If your chosen tile has a porous surface, it needs to be sealed to protect it.

> The floor surface needs to cope with dirt brought in by people or pets from outside.

> It's wise to choose a frost-proof flooring even in a conservatory, as these rooms can get cold in winter. If the flooring absorbs water and freezes, then sunlight first thing in the morning can cause it to crack.

> You can continue the tiles from your conservatory or porch to the outside for a seamless transition from home to garden. Remember to use frost-proof tiles if necessary for your climate.

types of tile

Tiles have been made from all kinds of materials over the years, from classic clays to modern porcelain and recycled glass. This section is a guide to the characteristics of the myriad of tile types, and how to get the most out of each one.

ceramic

Glazed ceramic tiles are the obvious choice for walls in bathrooms, kitchens and laundry areas. They are non-porous and hygienic and are very easy to clean. They will last a lifetime in most domestic environments and are one of the quickest and easiest ways to add value to your home.

When we first think of tiles, glazed tiles are often what we have in mind. They are the most tactile, just like beautiful fabrics. You want to run your fingers over them.

They are made initially from a blend of clays and fired at high temperatures. But this clay base is relatively unimpressive as far as the decorator is concerned. What sets these tiles apart is the glaze. After firing, the tiles are coated with a thin layer of raw materials which, on firing again, form a hard glass-like coating on the surface. In fact, the glaze, with all its tough and glossy qualities, can actually be considered to be a specialist form of glass.

▲ **Brighten up** Fun, designer ceramic tiles are a good way to lift the décor of the smallest room of the house.

Surface finishes

Glaze gives a tile its characteristic shiny finish, and also makes it non-porous. And there's an infinite variety of finished surfaces that can be created. Tiles can have a delicate, crackle finish; they may be optically smooth, slightly wavy and undulating, or the clay surface may have been left deliberately uneven to pool and hold the glaze, making magical shading effects.

Production techniques

Glazes are an art as well as a science, and many of the recipes for glazes are centuries old. But some have been lost altogether, leaving modern decorators wondering just how the craftsperson achieved such glowing and lustrous colours a thousand years ago. Although modern tiles come in a huge range of colours, some historic colours – the reds and turquoises of art deco tiling, for example – are unrepeatable because we no longer want to handle the dangerous chemicals that people once used to create them.

Clever glaze techniques mean that ceramic imitations of different stones and marbles abound, to make a stone or marble surface that is cheaper and easier to install than the real thing.

The bulk of ceramic tiles are machine made, but craft tiles are still made by hand in individual workshops and sold through suppliers who value the unique look of a tile that has been individually sculpted, glazed or painted. Hand-crafted tiles are understandably not made in huge numbers. They tend to have greater variation in colour and size, but this individuality is part of their appeal.

Influences

> Artists have always been fascinated by tiles and couldn't resist tackling this often difficult medium. Designers such as William Morris, Susie Cooper and William de Morgan produced ranges of tiles, some of which are still reproduced today.

> Modern designers are also producing editions of special, very personal tiles. These can be used to create a real talking point in your home, perhaps combined with a sympathetic background tile.

> Tile manufacturers are always experimenting with their raw materials. Environmentally friendly recycled ceramic tiles are now made from a mix of stone dust and recycled glass.

▲ **Array of colour** Inexpensive coloured single ceramic tiles have been mixed to create a bold multicoloured patchwork effect in this bathroom.

tile definitions

Transfer-printed tiles
A transfer design is applied to the surface of the tile in a similar way as to domestic china. The design doesn't have the depth or personality of one made by manipulating the glaze colours or by hand painting. Victorian tiles were often transfer printed and then hand painted in places to give them a little more character.

Sculpted tiles
Three-dimensional designs on the surface of tiles that are then left plain or painted, often by hand. Take care when grouting these kinds of tiles to avoid grout building up and settling in the crevices of the surface design.

Field tile
A plain tile used as the basic background in a tiling project.

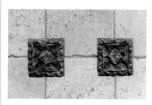

Accent tiles
More complex or elaborately decorated tiles that are used in small amounts as part of a tiling pattern to set off the field tile background. These accent tiles could be metallic, sculpted or glass tiles, or small, patterned inserts in a plain tiled floor.

Tube lining
A skilled method of decorating tiles developed in late Victorian times by piping the outline of the design onto each individual tile. The spaces left by the piping are then filled in by hand with coloured glazes.

Lustre
A pearlized finish that gives the tile an iridescent surface of subtle rainbow colours.

Borders
Bands of tiles to be used together with field tiles to finish off a tiling area, or to add shape and emphasis. Borders can be discreet changes of texture and shape, or a major design feature.

Mesh- or paper-backed tiles
Many small or mosaic tiles are now sold attached to a backing mesh or paper, ready-spaced for ease of installation. This makes final grouting easier and puts a mosaic-style project into the hands of a capable renovator.

Delft tiles

The original European tiling dating from the 17th century, with charming figures and motifs painted in blue on a white background. The practice of hand-making delft tiles (as opposed to machine-made imitations) has now been revived after its demise during the Industrial Revolution.

Special mouldings

Dados and trims that have been made to match the field tiles give a professional finish to a tiled area. Not all tile ranges have them, but some include bull nosing, frame or rail mouldings with internal and external corners, skirting tiles with internal and external corners, and quarter-round trim.

Encaustic tiles

These are produced by pouring liquid clay in contrasting colours into moulds to make a surface design, which is then given a clay or sand and cement backing. These kinds of tiles are porous until properly sealed and must be installed with care to avoid staining. True encaustic tiles are expensive because they have to be made by hand. You may be lucky, though, and find some reclaimed or secondhand. Some tiles copy the traditional encaustic designs, but close inspection reveals that they are just printed or painted onto the surface so will wear out in a few years. True encaustic tiles will survive for hundreds of years and still look good, because the design remains in the clay as the tile wears down. They are often combined in a floor with plainer geometric tiles that are less expensive.

Geometric floor tiles

These originated in churches, monasteries and the homes of the medieval wealthy. Small, simple geometric clay shapes are built up into an overall floor design of detailed, repeated patterns, which often have custom-shaped borders installed around the edge. The Victorians revived this style of flooring and used it in fancy hotels as well as in humble row houses, where these tiles can still be seen in entrance halls, porches, paths and doorways. Modern manufacturers have recreated these classic floor tiles and offer computer-aided designs so you can experiment with layouts and colour combinations and calculate quantities.

The colour goes right through this kind of tile, instead of just remaining on the surface. The natural colours (black, white, red, brown and buff) are less expensive than greens and blues, which are made by adding special stains to white clay.

The tiles are unglazed, so they need careful grouting to avoid staining the surface. They should also be sealed before the floor is used.

terracotta and saltillo

If you're unsure of what colour of flooring tile to choose, you can't go wrong with terracotta or Saltillo. Classics of the tile world, their warm colours fit in with contemporary furniture and more traditional interiors. Terracotta and Saltillo are very adaptable and can have borders or insert tiles added to them or can be used on their own.

terracotta

Terracotta is one of the oldest forms of tile flooring and has been used since ancient times. In this type of tile, the basic clay itself is the star of the show. Natural clay comes in a wide variety of rich, warm shades, from buff and beige to salmon pink and fox red, depending from which part of the world it originates. Each terracotta tile will be slightly different from the next, even within a single batch, and is sometimes tinged with black from its time in the kiln.

Terracotta tiles can be made by machine or molded by hand. Handmade terracotta tiles tend to have more character and variation but are expensive. Their finish can be relatively smooth or rough and irregular. Very adaptable, they can be set in a variety of patterns and used together with other tiles.

Terracotta tiles are fired at low temperatures, so they tend to be relatively matt in finish and porous. They must be thoroughly sealed once they have been laid, and they will often look different from the terracotta tiles on display in the showroom until this sealing is complete.

▲ **Spanish style** Terracotta tiling in all its forms combines well with carved wood and metalwork typical of Mediterranean décor.

saltillo

This type of tile is handmade in northern Mexico, and it is popular both because of its soft, hand-crafted appearance and relatively low cost, which means you can get a beautiful floor on a budget. They are typically a soft peachy-pink colour. This colour tends to be consistent across manufacturers, because they are all using the same clay from the same area of the world. They can only be used outside in climates where they won't encounter any frost, because they are sun-dried and fired at low temperatures. They are one of the thicker types of floor tile 0.5–2.5 cm (¼–1 inch) thick so take this into account when planning the subfloor and thresholds.

Quarry tiles

These are unglazed but fired at a high temperature, which makes them very hard wearing, though they also need to be sealed after fitting. Their classic small square shape is a traditional choice for kitchens, laundry rooms and work areas.

▲ **A taste of the Orient** Insert tiles and borders make perfect companions to terracotta tiling, giving a rich result reminiscent of an oriental carpet.

▼ **Sunken bath** Pale terracotta and Saltillo tiling form a natural link between indoors and out.

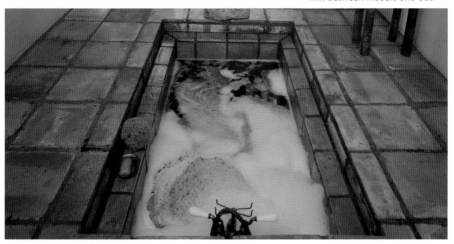

porcelain

The word porcelain conjures up images of delicate teacups, but as far as tiling goes, this couldn't be further from the truth. These tiles are tough and reliable. If you've got a large area to cover and want a dramatic finish without spending a fortune, then porcelain tiling is a sound choice.

A major advance of the last few years is porcelain tiles. You will probably have walked across a floor made of this discreet, tough material recently without realizing it, at your shopping mall or on the way to the office. The qualities that make porcelain tiling perfect for public places also make them good for the home. Now produced in factories all over the world and fired at very high temperatures, the main characteristics of porcelain tiles are their toughness, strength and very low water absorption. They can be glazed or unglazed, with a matt or shiny finish. They make excellent imitations of natural stone surfaces, only harder, more durable, easier to maintain and more stain resistant.

It can be very hard to tell the best porcelain-tile stone imitations from the real thing. With their subtle colouring and textures, the porcelain imitations can even mimic the slightly pitted finish of travertine.

▶ **Clever imitation** Porcelain tiling is available in superb faux versions of natural stone and slate.

Faking it

Working with real stone can be a challenge, so the advances in porcelain tiling make it a welcome alternative. You can acquire anything from a high-gloss finish to a rough, rocky texture with porcelain. And as far as sizes and colours go, these tiles are more reliable than real stone.

Porcelain tiles are readily available in large-size formats, which makes them good for large spaces. The sharp cut (rectified) edges means they can be close fitted, so grout lines are minimal and don't dominate the floor design.

The drawback of their extreme toughness, however, is that you need high-quality cutting and drilling equipment in order to work with them. This means you will probably have to hire professional tools if you aren't using a professional contractor.

▲ Terriffic textures
Porcelain tiling comes in a huge variety of surface finishes – a textured tile is the perfect contrast to natural woods.

◀ Sleek chic
This elegant modern poolside is typical of the way new porcelain tiling can achieve a unique, contemporary look.

stone

With its increasing availability, stone tiling in all its forms is becoming very popular for use all over the home. Stone is not just for floors – smaller tiling and mosaics are perfect for walls. Although stone is generally in natural and neutral colours, the detail and texture of its surface makes it interesting in any light. Stone tiling is also one of the quickest and easiest ways to add value to your home.

▲ **Renaissance style** Beautiful stone flags like these give any space an impression of effortless antiquity.

Tips

> Stone is naturally variable in colour and surface texture. A single sample of the stone may not be representative of the whole batch that is delivered to you. Ask to see a range of samples before making your choice.

> Stone tiles can vary slightly in size. This is considered normal in the trade.

> If you really want a consistent surface finish and colour, you would be happier with a manmade product like porcelain tiling.

> Stone is extremely heavy. It will probably be delivered in crates or pallets, and unless you arrange otherwise, it will be delivered to wherever the delivery truck is able to park. You may be able to make special arrangements to have it lifted to a more suitable position, but you can't expect the driver to carry it into the house for you.

> Some breakage is almost inevitable during shipping. You should complain to your supplier, however, if there has been extensive damage.

> The quarrying and cutting processes use a lot of water. Therefore, your stone may arrive damp and need to be dried out before use.

Once the prerogative of the wealthy and the aristocratic, stones and marbles have been chosen for hundreds, if not thousands, of years for grand architectural statements and memorials of national significance. Recent advances in production methods means that these beautiful materials are now available to everyone, in an ever-widening number of colours and finishes. Stone and marble create distinctive and serene interiors with a great sense of permanence. Their hardness makes them highly suitable for flooring, where they will last for generations if well cared for.

Style
Stone flooring used to be associated with a country farmhouse style, but now it is part of contemporary urban chic as well. Stone is especially sympathetic to antique furniture and old textiles, but it looks equally stunning in a modern interior.

Increasingly popular throughout the home, natural stone is becoming more affordable due to improved quarrying and processing techniques. The main problem now is being spoiled for choice. Where dealers used to have a limited palette of colours, they can now show a huge range of fascinating marbles and granites, from calm and classic neutrals to unusual and distinctive stones of immense character.

Availability
Stone is available for walls and floors as individual tiles in all sizes and as mesh-backed mosaics.

Some companies specialize in reclaiming old stone floors. They prepare them for you to re-lay, so you can buy a piece of hundred-year-old history to cover your new kitchen floor.

◀ **Classically cool** Marble tiles have been used throughout this gleaming bathroom, including in the sunken shower area.

types of stone

Granite is one of the hardest stones available and comes in colours ranging from coal black to cloud grey, as well as reds and greens, with a characteristic speckled and dappled pattern. Usually polished or honed, granite looks best in a large-tile format to minimize grout lines. Although tough, it is prone to staining and may need sealing.

Marble starts its life as limestone and is then transformed by geological processes into a much harder, more crystalline rock. It's typically veined on top of mixed background colours. The veins can be contrasting and striking or light cobwebs of fine lines.

Sandstone is a sedimentary rock, like limestone, but formed mainly of quartz, which gives it its glossy look. Finely textured, sandstones tend to be pervious to water, so you'll have to find suitable places to use them.

Limestone comes in a huge range of neutral colours, from beige and buttermilk to nearly white and off-white, and tan and grey-blue. Close inspection sometimes reveals minute fossils and shells in the surface, which adds to the charm of this stone. Limestone is vulnerable to acids – including lemon juice – and some cleaning materials.

Travertine is a limestone formed near a hot spring where the water or gasses created this stone's characteristic pitted surface. It has a luxurious, silky feel and a soft, slightly matt finish. Travertine is found in colours like honey, buff, cream and rich bronzes. The naturally holey surface can make it unsuitable for kitchen countertops or bathrooms. Filled travertine has been given a smooth and level surface in the factory by filling the holes with a mixture of resin and stone powder.

types of finishes

Polished: A shiny and reflective finish. The harder stones, such as marble and granite, take this finish best.

Honed: A softer, satin finish usually seen on limestones and travertines.

Tumbled: A rustic, aged appearance created by "tumbling" the stones to soften the edges.

Cleft: The stone is split and left with the natural cleft marks, rather than being cut smoothly by a saw. Slate is typically a cleft stone.

Bush hammered: A rough surface created by beating the stone with a pointed hammer.

Brushed: A weathered look is achieved by using a rotary-wire brush on the surface of the stone.

Sandblasted: A rough surface texture created by blasting the stone with a stream of sand particles. This gives a slightly roughened finish that is not as uneven as the other irregular finishes.

Flamed: The surface of the stone is given a rough finish by exposing it to high heat.

▲ **Polished mixture** Simply combining a stone tile in a polished finish with a less reflective one can form the basis of a tile pattern.

▲ **Rough and tumble** Stone can be left with a natural rustic finish, which can also be artificially created using hammering and brushing techniques.

stone tile edges

Diamond sawn: A clean-cut edge made by a machine.

Chiselled or chipped edge: An uneven, rustic finish added to the edge after the stone has been cut.

Tumbled edge: Tiles are rolled around in a drum to create softer edges and corners.

Bevelled edge: The edge of the tile is cut off at an angle to make a smoother finish after grouting.

Honed and filled: The tile surface is filled during production to give a smooth finish.

slate

Slate can look charming and rustic or very modern indeed. European and American slates tend toward the softer, natural shades, while slates from the Far East and Brazil can have extraordinary hues of blue, copper, purple and salmon pink. African slates can be particularly dark and dramatic, with rich highlights and veins of coloured minerals.

Slates always give a rich, earthy effect, and the almost black versions look stunning in modern interiors.

slate finishes

Calibrated: Tiles are machined to an equal thickness on both sides. These are the easiest types of slate tile to install.

Gauged: Machined on the underside to give a consistent thickness, the face of the slate retains its natural state.

Guillotine cut: Using a chopping method, textured and irregular edges are created on the tile.

Random flags: This technique makes a collection of different sized tiles, which will need care and thought in planning and placing.

Ungauged: Both sides of the tile are left in their natural cleft state. The thickness may vary. You need a skilled installer to lay these tiles.

▲ **Modern magic** Contemporary slate and stone give a perfect background for sleek furniture, as in this dining room.

▲ **Country life** Stone and slate make excellent entranceways, where muddy boots and shoes are coming in and out.

▶ **Pebble floors** are fun surfaces made of pebbles, matched for colour and size and closely set on a backing material ready to be laid as tiles. Grouting reduces the bumpy surface to something more appropriate to walk on, but they are never going to appeal to everyone. More practical are pebble tiles where the pebbles have been set deep into transparent or translucent coloured resin to make a fascinating tile that is perfectly smooth underfoot.

◀ **Convenient versatility** Stone tile squares make a useful splashback for this basin. Stone is available in small formats and warm colours, which makes it very versatile.

costing the earth?

Lower production costs overseas can mean less expensive stone and granite tiles.

However, there's often a hidden price being paid in the quarries – child or bonded labour, low health and safety standards, and little concern for the environment can all be factors in manufacturing these seemingly inexpensive tiles.

Traceability of an individual stone is difficult – it's often impossible for the consumer to be sure of the source. Boycotting suppliers can result in taking work away from desperately poor people; so perhaps the most useful thing to do is maintain the pressure at this end of the supply chain for ethical sourcing.

▶ **Modern minimalism** Stone flooring always looks luxurious, even in settings of architectural simplicity.

▲ **Impressive entrances** An exquisite geometric flooring pattern, made up of beautifully contrasting stone and marble pieces, is a timeless classic.

▲ **Natural setting** This sink has been set into a surround made of stone tiling in a variety of natural colours.

glass

Glass is a material that is increasingly being used by designers and manufacturers to bring light and space into our homes. By reflecting light, glass tiling gives a unique and eye-catching finish. Whether it is in a simple colour or more complex rainbow glass mosaic, it needs a little extra care when installing but is tough enough, when properly used, for floors as well as walls.

Glass tiles have a unique lustrous quality and are very touchable. They appear luminous, apparently glowing from within, and make the most of available light by reflecting it back into the room. In a range of colours based around greens, blues, browns and whites, they can have earth oxides or metal foils added to their mix to create tiles that glisten in the light with a beautiful iridescence, reminiscent of Byzantine mosaics.

Smalti tiles
Created by pouring molten glass into trays and allowing it to cool, these tiles have a characteristic cloudy finish and were the original type of glass used in Byzantine mosaics, often combined with gold leaf. They are available as mesh-backed mosaic for modern use.

▶ **Glowing**
Good lighting in a room is essential to bring out the full beauty of iridescent glass tiling.

Recycled glass

Tiles made from recycled glass are both environmentally friendly and extremely functional, being very tough and strong. Recycled glass makes a semitransparent or opaque tile with marble-like patterns that vary depending on the type of glass used (e.g. whether it's from old bottles or recycled car windows).

Glass on the floor

Glass floor tiles maximize light by reflecting it rather than absorbing it. Like ceramic tiles, glass tiles will shatter if they are hammered or subject to a violent impact. Only choose tiles that are specifically rated for use on floors. Smalti small glass floor tiles have a cloudy, rough texture that protects against slips and falls. Glass mosaic and small-format glass tiles provide slip protection because of the high frequency of tile edges and grout lines. Translucent and large-format glass tiles need an etched or textured surface to qualify as non-slip. Like glossy ceramic tiles, they become very slippery when wet.

Installation

Take care when installing glass tiles. Floor tiles, in particular, are usually set with a flexible adhesive against a crack-suppression membrane. There needs to be a complete layer of adhesive under the tile because anything less will show through to the surface under translucent glass tiles. It's also important that no pockets of air are trapped under the tiles. This could weaken and eventually crack the tiles as they are walked on. To prevent this, the backs of the tiles are usually buttered with adhesive as they are laid.

▲ **Ideal match** Glass tiling has a natural affinity with anything else made of glass, so this fine orange tiling works well with the plain frost of the shower door.

Tips

> Glass tiling can be used inside or out, in hot or cold temperatures, and in both wet and dry locations.

> Glass tiles are very tough. They withstand water and chemicals and do not fade.

> They can be used to cover an entire surface or blended with other tile finishes.

> There is a huge variety of finishes for glass tiles – from translucent to textured, jewel-like to opalescent.

> Generally, the thicker the tile, the more intense the colour. Standard glass tile thicknesses are from 4–8 mm ($\frac{1}{3}$–$\frac{1}{4}$ inch). Thinner tiles tend to break during shipping and handling.

> To realize the full effect of some of the iridescent finishes, you may need to change the lighting in your room.

> Glass mosaic tiling is extremely popular and comes in a wide range of individual or mixed colours.

metallic

Metals have always been highly valued for their sense of permanence and strength. The shine of metals, from bright gold to gentle silvers and platinum, is available in a wide range of tiles, which you can use either to make a bold statement or to add a clever counterpoint to an area of plainer tiles.

Once fairly rare as a finish for decorating, the gleam of metal, from opulent brass, gold or copper colours to cooler silver, steel and platinum, is now available in tile surfaces. Metallic is more the name of a finish than an actual tile. These metallic tiles can range from real cast metal to a resin or ceramic tile body that has been given a metal coating. It's easy to tell all these apart by simply looking at the back of the tile. Some metallic finishes are simply a clever glaze that gives the impression of hammered metal.

▶ **Metallic gleam** Although it would need regular cleaning to keep its shine, a metal mosaic complements the metal sink elements in this bathroom.

Tips

> Metallic tiles can be installed over a large area, but they also look good as an accent tile. They mix well with stones.

> Metallic finishes are effective when included in fireplaces and kitchen splashbacks.

> Usually light-reflecting, metallics lend importance to any surface. They also make a pattern stand out vividly.

> The effect produced by using metallic tiles can be strong, so use them with caution. The cooler metallics, in particular, can have an almost icy feel.

> Metallic glazes may not be as resistant to mild acids – like lemon juice and some cleaning materials – as a pure metal. They are recommended for dry areas only.

▲ **Metallic mix** The bronze accent tiles here are complemented by the jade green; and the bronze mix in some of the other tiles adds further interest.

mosaic and picture tiles

The increasing availability of mosaic and picture tiles has facilitated the creation of individual patterns on walls and floors. If you like the idea of adding a personal touch to a room, then use one of the many companies that will make picture tiles to order or supply mosaic pictures in all colours and sizes.

Ancient mosaics were labour intensive, built by hand out of many little pieces of marble and precious stone, taking months to complete. But the latest production techniques mean mosaics are accessible to even the laziest of modern decorators. Ready-formed mosaics set onto tiling sheets in subtly mixed shades of a single colour band, patterns and medallions are readily available for purchase. The tile designers and manufacturers have done all the tricky work for you. All you have to do is lay them with a little care and grout.

Digitally printed tiles
Digital technology means that you can have a custom design printed on ceramic tiles. This could be an individual photo on a single tile, a custom-made mural or a wall design.

▶ **Custom mosaic** Modern mosaic artists can reproduce any picture with painstaking photographic accuracy, creating a modern work of art from thousands of tiny pieces of marble and stone.

Tips

> Grout lines are very prominent in mosaic tiling, so make sure that you choose the right colour of grout.

> Use an installer who is experienced in handling mosaic tiles. The sheets must be aligned correctly to make the joins invisible.

> Mosaics come in as many varieties of finishes as single tiles, with sharp or tumbled and chipped edges.

> Mosaic tiles can create a beautiful small-tile surface. However, there are also more complex mosaic designs, inspired by ancient Roman or Moorish designs, for larger areas.

> Ready-made mosaic medallions will make a gorgeous centrepiece in a floor set with a simple, less expensive field tile.

> Borders in classical mosaic motifs, such as the wave, the Greek key or the rope design, bring a touch of historic grandeur to a bathroom.

◀ **Short cut** A mosaic flooring design can be bought ready-made from a specialist company, or you can design your own based on modern, convenient mesh-backed mosaic.

▶ **Bold and beautiful** This large fish mosaic is perfectly offset by the simplicity of the plain blue mosaic that completely surrounds it in the rest of the bathroom.

antique

Antique tiles are visually appealing. Manufactured in the millions during the 19th century in particular, the best have survived and can be found with a little diligent searching. Tile collectors' clubs snap up the most desirable tiles quickly, but even if you only find a few beautiful antiques, they can be combined with modern tiles to stunning effect.

▶ **Quality with age** If you only have a few original antique tiles, you could use them in accessories, such as this Victorian planter.

Tips

> Don't be afraid to mix old and new. Tile sizes haven't changed much over the years, so a few beautiful antique tiles can be set easily into a simple background of modern tiles to make a kitchen splashback, for example.

> Antique tiles are usually thicker than modern ones, so lay them first and bring the level of the modern tiles up to match them.

> Individual antique tiles look good framed and hung singly or in groups.

> Antique tiles can be set into wood or brass frames to make stands for flowerpots, teapots and anything else that might damage a fine wood surface.

> Many people enjoy collecting both antique and modern tiles on a particular theme – like animals or flowers – to decorate their home.

Salvage yards

> Wear sturdy shoes or boots when you visit a salvage yard. Take gloves so that you can dig in and get a really good look.

> At a salvage yard, there are likely to be fewer staff available to answer your questions than at a ritzy showroom. You will have to be enterprising.

> Be prepared to take all the information you need. If you go home to check the measurements of a great find, it may be gone by the time you return. It's unlikely you'll be able to match found tiles with another supplier, so you have to think on your feet and be decisive.

Using antique tiles is the ultimate way to recycle. Tiles will often outlast the buildings they were first used in, and many companies specialize in the reclamation of both stone and terracotta floors from around the world. They preserve these beautifully aged materials for reuse in modern building.

Larger-scale projects

If you are energetic, then salvaging old tiles can be extremely satisfying. If your budget is limited, you may be able to buy better quality tiles secondhand than if you hold out for new. Reclamation yards often have salvaged stone flooring, bricks and terracotta tiles available.

 Floral fancies William de Morgan worked at the very end of the 19th century, producing tile designs that are still sought after today. These sculpted naturalistic flowers are typical of his craftsmanship.

 The test of time
Encaustic tiling of this quality and craftsmanship lasts for hundreds of years. Specialist companies can clean and restore a well-trodden area of encaustic tiling to its former glory.

CLEANING ANTIQUE TILES

> Avoid any excessive cleaning treatments. Don't soak them – if water gets behind the glaze, it will lift it right off the tile.

> Use a little water and a soft cloth to remove dirt.

> The pan scrubber of a sponge can be used to gently clean the antique tile, if necessary. Try to avoid steel wool.

> Polish the glaze with a soft cloth. Once clean, all the tiles need is an occasional dusting.

cork and leather

Cork and leather are both natural materials, but they couldn't be more different when it comes to tiling. Leather tiles are the ultimate luxury floor and wall covering, needing a degree of care to prevent damage once they are laid. Cork, however, is perfect for the family home – an ideal surface for children to play on.

▲ **Luxurious leather** Leather floor tiling can be manufactured in complex designs like this one, matching the furniture and desktops.

Cork tips

> Cork has unique qualities of elasticity, thermal insulation and sound reduction. It is a honeycomb of millions of tiny cells. Each one of these cells functions as a miniature shock absorber.

> These individual cells also make it a very resilient and comfortable flooring. Although it is soft, minor dents (made by dropped toys, for example) will bounce back.

> Cork is not as resistant to abrasion as linoleum or vinyl. It's not suitable for very high-traffic areas.

> Cork is good in bathrooms because it is resilient and warm underfoot. Water-proof, ready-sealed cork tiles are available, but you still need to apply a coat of sealant to seal the joints after the floor is laid.

> Although usually available in warm, natural colours, cork takes coloured stains as well.

> Like any natural material, it tends to fade a little over time where exposed to light.

> Areas that get the most traffic will need to have the sealing or varnish renewed from time to time where the cork has become worn.

> For floors, make sure the tiles are flooring grade. Don't purchase wall cork by mistake.

cork

A renewable resource, cork is harvested from trees that are up to 200 years old. Cork bark is cut every nine years or so, without killing the tree. In Portugal, Spain, Corsica, Sardinia and Italy, sustainable cork forests form a valuable habitat for rare wildlife. Renewed interest in environmentally friendly materials has also renewed interest in cork. It is being produced to higher standards now than ever before.

leather

Leather floor and wall tiles give an air of unabashed luxury. Sensual and organic, leather gives any space a feeling of sophistication. Leather feels warm and soft and ages beautifully, developing a rich patina if well looked after. For a special room that is going to be treated with care, leather is a wonderful choice – if you have the budget, that is.

▲ **Protective placement** Leather tiling on walls is less likely to be damaged than tiles on floors, though care must be taken with furniture backs that may rub against it.

Leather tips

> Leather is a natural fibre that will be affected by water and moisture, so it isn't suitable for areas like bathrooms or kitchens.

> Made from the strongest, thickest, most central part of the hide, leather is expensive to produce.

> Colours vary naturally between batches. Make sure you order the correct number of leather tiles at the beginning because it may be impossible to match later.

> Lay out the tiles to view them before you stick them down. You may want to reposition some of them to balance the variations in tile colour.

> Leather is a relatively expensive flooring to install because the subfloor needs to be excellent.

> As it's quite a new material for flooring, you may have difficulty finding a leather tiler in your area.

> To reduce any risk of shrinkage, it's best to let the tiles acclimatize in the room for four or five days before laying them down.

> Leather can fade on prolonged exposure to sunlight. Consider light curtains on the windows to protect the tiles in a bright south- or west-facing room.

> On the floor, leather tiles need regular waxing to keep them water resistant.

linoleum, vinyl, rubber

The big advantage to using linoleum, vinyl and rubber tiles is their low cost and easy handling. The added bonus is that you are still able to create designs and patterns, as with ceramic tiles.

linoleum

Like cork, linoleum is another environmentally friendly floor covering that is being seriously reconsidered. Made of boiled linseed oil, pine resin, wood flour and ground limestone on a woven jute backing, it was invented over a hundred years ago. Not only is linoleum easy to clean, but it is biodegradable and made from harvestable sources.

vinyl

For many years, vinyl has been the unquestioned choice for inexpensive, functional flooring, particularly in demanding areas like kitchens and bathrooms. Thin, poor quality vinyls in cheap designs, however, have given this material a bad name. If you are prepared to pay just a little more, excellent-quality vinyls are available. Top-of-the-line vinyl tiles with photographic-quality wood and stone effects are much in demand.

rubber

This material can take a lot of punishment and has been used for many years in commercial properties like airports and gymnasiums. Rubber tiles give a contemporary, sometimes industrial look, but in clear, bright colours they can add fun and style to a family kitchen or playroom.

Linoleum tips

> Linoleum is easy to install, resilient and comfortable underfoot. It's durable enough for high-traffic areas.

> Naturally anti-bacterial, linoleum tiles have been used for many years in clinics and hospitals.

> The colour in linoleum doesn't fade quickly because it isn't just a surface application, it travels right through to the back of the tile.

> Linoleum is available in classic, muted colours and marble designs, as well as bright contemporary colours like lime green and cobalt blue.

> Although more expensive than standard vinyl, linoleum has a longer life.

> Linoleum tiles can be laid in patterns or chequered styles like any other tile. You can also commission a custom-made design using CAD technology.

> Marmoleum is one brand name for linoleum, but there are several manufacturers operating around the world.

Vinyl tips

> Even the better ranges of vinyl floor tiles are inexpensive compared with other floorings. They come in a huge assortment of colours and are easy to install.

> Many vinyl tiles are uncanny imitations of stones and ceramics. They are warmer to the touch than true ceramic, and they obviously aren't prone to cracking or developing dirty grout lines in quite the same way as stone.

> Vinyl tiles are made of a synthetic material called polyvinyl chloride (PVC). Because they can give off potentially harmful toxins and are not biodegradable, the tiles unfortunately can't be recycled at the end of their useful life.

> Peel-and-stick versions of vinyl tiles can be found easily, but it's worth it to pay for a substantial vinyl rather than a thin, flimsy one.

> In the more expensive ranges, you can add mosaic-, border-, metallic- or pebble-style strips into the design mix.

Rubber tips

> Some rubber tiles are made entirely of natural rubber, a renewable resource from rubber trees. Others are a mixture of natural rubber and a synthetic. Recycled car tires are being used to make rubber floors, though mainly for sports surfaces at the moment.

> Rubber absorbs impact noise, is non-slip, stable and cigarette-burn resistant.

> With its slip and water resistance, rubber is an excellent choice for bathrooms. If used for a shower, you'll need a system installed beneath the tiles to prevent water leakage.

> Rubber is not the ideal choice for kitchens. Grease spills can make rubber tiles hazardous, and dirt can accumulate in studded rubber textures.

> Rubber comes in plain colours, marbleized finishes or a terrazzo style with all sorts of colours and densities of chip patterns. Manufacturers haven't been able to produce a successful white rubber – it tends to be a dirty chewing-gum colour – but other pale colours are readily available.

> Surface textures such as dots, diamonds or waves are available in rubber, as is a highly polished finish that reflects light.

> Rubber tiles are suitable for use with appropriate under-floor heating (but not one designed for use with ceramic tiles, which grows too hot).

> It's not advisable to use rubber tiles outdoors because the colours can fade unless specially treated.

> Rubber tiles are generally stuck down with adhesive, but you can also source loose-lay interlocking jigsaw tiles. It's then easy to replace single tiles in the event of damage.

tile directory

The directory is your guide to the stunning range of tiles available, organized by colour. There's advice on colour choice and suggestions for schemes based on your tile selection. The letters "W" and/or "F" at the end of each description indicate whether the tile is most suited to walls (W) and/or floors (F).

red

Red is an uncompromising colour. Energetic, vibrant and glowing, it is the most attention-grabbing colour in the spectrum. Associated with energy and vitality, it also has associations with aggression and danger, which can make it a colour that has to be used with care and discretion. Hot reds have the most dramatic impact, whilst softer reds, such as fuchsia and magenta, are more passionate and romantic. Its palest version – pink – suggests affection and femininity.

red

Reds are advancing colours – they appear to come toward you and make a space look smaller, warmer and more welcoming. However, bright reds used indiscriminately can be claustrophobic and overstimulating. Reds are, therefore, best for rooms that are not used all the time, such as a dining room. A strong hue gives an attractive ambience under soft lighting or candlelight but is less attractive in bright daylight when it can seem oppressive.

Green is the complementary colour to red, and using the two together can make a stimulating scheme that would be suited to a family bathroom or hallway. The softer versions of sage green and plaster pink make for a much gentler scheme suitable for bedrooms.

Rich purples are next to red on the colour wheel, and with them are the strongest of the advancing colours. Purples can be used to visually decrease the size of a room and make it more welcoming. Their paler versions, blue-pinks and violets, suggest well-being and sensuality.

Red's complementary colour is green. Purple's complementary colour is yellow.

▲ Cheerful red tiling is a classic for a kitchen splashback, along a work counter.

▲ Red is an unusual colour to choose for a bathroom,
but when done with confidence, it will always impress.

 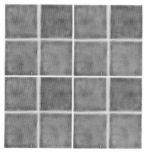 

▲ **Corals and pinks** These mosaic tiles in a variety of coral shades have a vibrancy due to the dappled effect of the surface glazes. Large areas of these tiles will never look plain, as they always have an interesting texture to them. Suitable colours to combine with them would be coffee browns and taupes, or warm greys. W

▲ **Top band** This tile includes a banded top that could be used to finish off a tile area without using an additional border. W

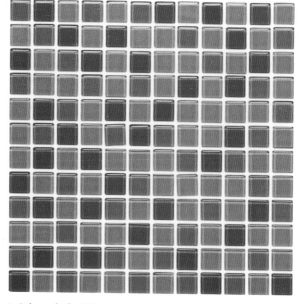

▲ **Colour clash** Bright orange and pink are an unusual colour combination but work beautifully in this stunning mosaic. W

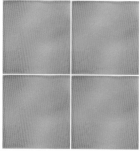

▲ **Pretty in pink** A tile in a glowing sugar pink that would look great combined with white in a bathroom. W

▲ **Border combination**
A simple edge tile in the same colour finishes off this run of coral tiles. Note the matching grout. W

▲ **Brick tiles** Whether large or small, horizontal tiles lead the eye around the room. W

▲ **Café au lait** Turquoise blue would make a good contrast to this sophisticated tile, which could be used both horizontally and vertically. W

▲ **Linoleum** Modern linoleum tiling comes in a wide range of colours, including this warm pink and beige combination. W/F

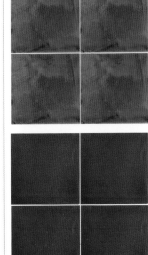

▲ **Traditional colours** These tiles in rich red and purple would be a favourite in the 19th century where dark, glowing colours were used everywhere with great confidence. W

▲ **Jewel bright** Inexpensive glass mosaic tiles can easily resemble precious stones, such as garnet or ruby. Their ability to pick up light and reflect it back gives them a glowing quality, as if lit from within. W

▲ **Orange stars** Children would love a design like this, which would cheer up a light-starved room. W

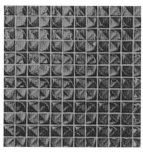

▲ **Gentle red** Red tiles needn't be strident but can have a soft, textured finish like this glass mosaic. W

▲ **Dragged lines** This tile design imitates the fine, elegant lines of the popular dragged-paint finish. W

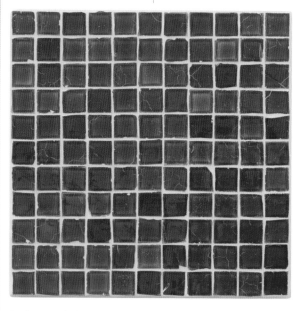

▲ **Cherry red** These glass tiles use almost transparent glass in a range of cherry red shades. W

▲ **Toning colors** Use a colour mixture in a mosaic tile to create the colour scheme for the rest of the room. W

▲ **Using mosaic strips** Mosaic strips are very versatile and can be used both as inserts on the wall and for edging shelves, windowsills and other places where the tiles change direction. W

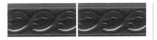

▲ **Imperial purple** A classic border design in a dark wine purple. W

▲ **Shades of blue** Here dark purple has been combined with fresher blues to lighten the overall effect. W

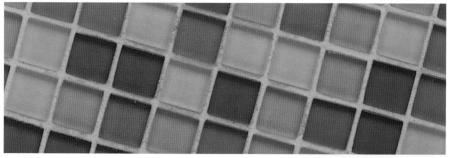

▲ **Graded pinks** The colours in this pink glass mosaic shade from a clear blue-pink to a warmer orange-pink, giving lots of flexibility in building a colour scheme around them. W

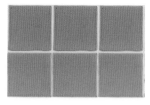

▲ **Simple colour** If you are wary of using bright pinks, then this soft plaster pink is a sound choice. W

▲ **Natural look** The hand-crafted feel of these earthy terracotta tiles is perfect for warming a modern kitchen. W

▲ **Dark colour** If you want a really deep-coloured tile, then this maroon glaze would be perfect. W

▲ **Tangerine** Burnt tangerine looks great with dark browns as well as lighter naturals. W

▲ **Large-scale panel** A large mosaic panel can be custom-made for walls or floors. W/F

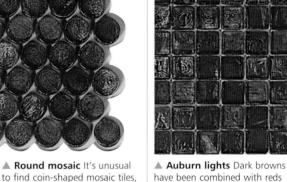

▲ **Round mosaic** It's unusual to find coin-shaped mosaic tiles, but they are fixed and grouted in just the same way as square mosaics. W/F

▲ **Auburn lights** Dark browns have been combined with reds here for an overall effect of rich, glowing bronze. W

▲ **Taking turns** Translucent glass mosaic is alternated with a matt, opaque tile, giving a jewel-studded effect. W

▲ **Pretty inserts** Softly coloured inserts are used as decorative bands and borders between lines of larger tiles. W

▲ **Retro swirls** Mosaic tiles are perfect for creating bold swirling designs within an otherwise straight-tiled area. W/F

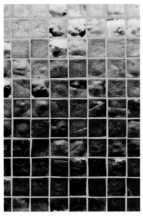

▲ **Coral mosaic** Coral red is an unusual colour for schemes but is worth considering instead of more conventional pinks. W

▲ **Complementary colours** This red-purple mosaic contains shades of complementary green, which could be used to build a contrasting colour scheme. W

▲ **Blending colours** In this mosaic, pink is combined with colours close to it on the colour wheel, giving an overall effect of warmth. W

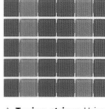

▲ **Toning stripes** Using two slightly different tones of a similar colour creates interest without being overpowering. W

▲ **Purples and blues** Note how carefully the grout here has been colour matched for a top-notch finish. W

▲ **Subdued red** Red can be toned down, giving a room a totally different ambience from one decorated in a bright primary hue. W

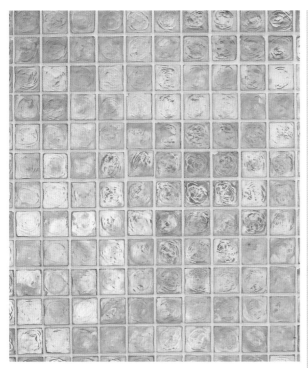

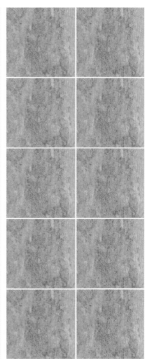

▲ **Rainbow shimmer** The exquisite colouring of this mosaic needs an understated scheme built around it, so that it is not swamped. W

▲ **Background pink** Simple textured tiles form a solid background to much brighter versions of the same colours. W

Ecological choice Natural linoleum, also known as Marmoleum, is a durable floor covering made from sustainable, biodegradable materials. Available in an exciting array of colours, such as the three shown above. They make a strong stand-alone accent or, used together, a bold design statement. W/F

▲ **Deckchair** Detailed picture tiles should be fixed at around eye level – children's eye level is especially effective. W

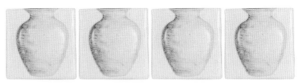

▲ **Terracotta pot** Motif tiles can be repeated as a short border or used singly. W

▲ **Mixed-format borders** Mixing marble, glass, tile or pebble in a border gives a unique, arty look. W

▲ **Mosaic border** Ready-made borders like this work well with both stone and brighter terracotta. W/F

▲ **Frog** This fun tile is an example of craftsmanship by the tile painter and would be suitable as a bathroom border. W

Motif tiles To be truly appreciated, these beautifully crafted and painted tiles should be used sparingly, within a background of plainer tiles. Most motif tiles come with a matching field tile specifically for this purpose. Sculpted tiles are particularly fascinating and appealing to the touch. W

Drawn from nature Flowers and butterflies have always been inspiration for tile art. You can mix and match tiles like these, as long as the size and background colour are the same. They are perfect for giving a small tiled area a touch of individuality, where only one or two motifs are needed. The leaf skeleton motif has a cooler, more contemporary feel than flowers or fruit, but it could be used in exactly the same way. W

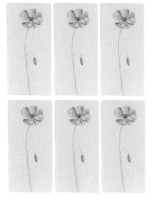

Motif tiles in larger spaces In a large tiled area where single motif tiles could look a little lost, take the opportunity to use larger motif plaques as a feature point. Alternatively, you can use repeated groups of motif tiles, making a larger statement and balancing the bigger background. This could be groups of the same tiles, or groups of different tiles from the same range would be equally effective. W

Red hallway Here the rich red-based tones of this elaborate geometric flooring design have been brought out in the wall colour, making a very welcoming hallway. As in the tiles here, a touch of sky blue is often used as a cool counterpoint colour, which can also be a link to the decoration of rooms beyond. F

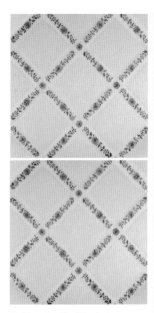

▲ **Red lozenge** This unusual red lozenge shape in a geometric border would make a striking contrast to a plain centre panel. W/F

▲ **Rose trellis** Tile designs like this have a big impact over a large area despite their simplicity, so try them out before you buy. W

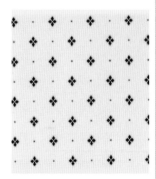

▲ **Powder motif** This classical sprinkling of a small motif over a tile gives a pretty overall effect on a wall; combine it with a stronger border design. W

▲ **Botanical panel** Use a detailed panel just as you would hang a picture, taking care over the positioning and making it the focus of the wall. W

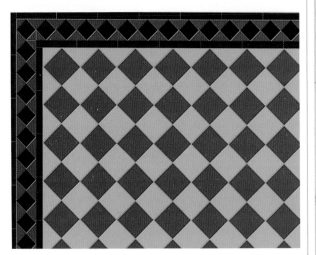

Geometric designs These three flooring designs show how different and complex patterns can be built up from simple tile shapes using only a limited palette of colours. The lower design uses only squares and triangles and a simple band to great effect. During the Victorian era, red, buff and black were the classic combination, whilst blues tended to be used less often as they were a more expensive tile. F

▲ **Vertical panel** Traditionally used either side of a fireplace, original versions of these panels are particularly sought after. This is a modern reproduction. W

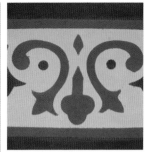

▲ **Victorian style** Strong repeating tile patterns were popular in the 19th century, often used to cover large areas or placed as repeating panels within plain tiles and borders along hallways. The Gothic style also used these bold patterns on floors, especially in halls and conservatories. W/F

▲ **True encaustic** A real encaustic tile is created out of coloured liquid clays, giving a characteristic outline to the motifs. W/F

▲ **Floral extravaganza** Bright and eye-catching flower tile panels make a wonderful centrepiece on a bathroom or kitchen wall. W

▲ **Edwardian beauty** Images of elegant women were a popular theme in early 20th-century decoration, including tile panels. W

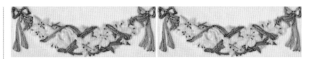

▲ **Flowery swags** These could be used individually or to create a border at picture-rail moulding level. W

▲ **Victorian classic** A classic border design in a rich brown-red – perfect combined with traditional cream. W

Transfer-print tiles These four tiles are modern reproductions of a very common traditional tile, where a sepia-coloured transfer design was first applied to the surface. This was then hand painted – the better quality tiles showing brighter colours in a wider range than the cheaper ones. These tiles are often seen in a mix-and-match combination around fireplaces in humbler homes or forming panels on the walls of door porches in Victorian housing. W

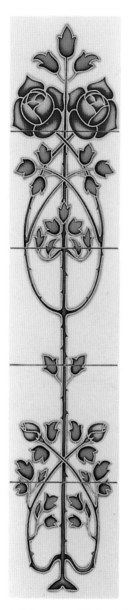

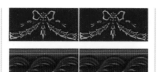

▲ **Traditional borders** Borders like these would have been commonly used with field tiles of the same colour, which would often cover a whole wall in a kitchen or bathroom, giving a very strong, enclosed feel. W

▲ **Exquisite roses** The soft sage green in this border tile could be picked out as a contrast colour in the room. W

▲ **Rope border** The rope border design always looks good and brings a masculine touch to a bathroom. W

▲ **Floral trim** For added impact, create running friezes that combine floral flat border tiles (in the centre) with three-dimensional moulded trims (sandwiching the floral tiles), such as the rope border above. W

▲ **Art nouveau** The inspiration for this panel is the stylized use of stems and flowers typical of the art nouveau movement. W

▲ **Goddess** This tile panel has a semi-mythical theme, reminiscent of the late 19th century. W

▲ **Nouveau border** Sinuous shapes based on nature were used by art nouveau designers. W

▲ **Lilac glass** These glass tiles are an example of the more unusual shapes available. W

▲ **Designer glass** A design classic that shows off the designer's expertise, with floating inserts of colour in a translucent glass base. W

▲ **Contemporary stripes** Designer tiles with candy pink stripes combine with a bold black to make a statement. W

▲ **Diamond border** A border like this is a good way of adding a touch of colour to neutral tiling. W/F

▲ **Random mosaic** Red and green are classic complementary colours – here a burgundy-red is combined with a grey-green. W

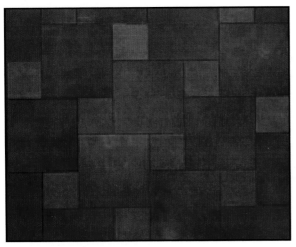

▲ **Red leather** Leather takes dyes very well, and these pinky-red tiles have been laid in a design using two different sizes. W/F

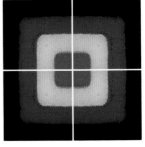

▲ **Red and black design** An example of how a single tile can form a more complex design, which can then be repeated. W

▲ **Digital print** Some incredible colours and effects can be printed onto tiles using state-of-the-art digital technology. W

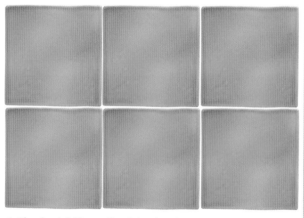

▲ **Classic pink** The quality of the glaze here gives this otherwise simple tile a luxurious-looking finish. W

▲ **Pink print** A large overall design is built up from these tiles, making an excellent single wall surface, with plainer tiles elsewhere to set it off. W

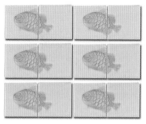

▲ **Fish tiles** A small, fun motif on a contemporary tile shape. W

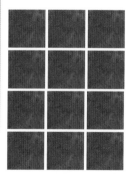

▲ **Coloured cork** The variations of shade in coloured cork add interest and depth with a marble-effect pattern. W/F

orange

Orange is one of the warmest colours – almost as intense and advancing as red – and can be quite strident if used on its own. Pure orange should mostly be confined to smaller surfaces or as an accent colour. Softer versions of orange (such as apricot, melon and terracotta) are warm and welcoming, and form some of the most popular tile colours.

orange

Orange is the colour of earth, so it's not surprising that many floor tiles are based on this colour, though this can range from an orange that is almost dark brown to a pale cream with just a hint of orange warmth.

Naturally, orange is prevalent in autumn, which suggests its association with fruitfulness and plenty. Perhaps this is why it is a suitable colour choice for dining rooms, giving a warm positive glow without the stridency of red.

Orange is an effective combiner – it sits beautifully with natural stone and wood colours, and forms a perfect companion to neutrals.

For a stronger scheme, giving a more punchy, Mediterranean feel, try combining orange with its complementary colour, blue. A dramatic blue-grey slate or stone flooring will be complemented by using a soft orange-based colour in the rest of the room, which will bring out the flooring colours without fighting for dominance.

Cold rooms can be transformed using orange in all its variety, together with the other warm colours based on yellows and reds. And if you need a colour to lift a cool, modern kitchen based around granite and metallic finishes, a coral or pale orange will add warmth but still keep a contemporary feel.

Orange's complementary colour is blue.

▲ An earthy orange has been chosen for this bathroom, and the smart white grouting lines pick up perfectly on the white basin and walls above.

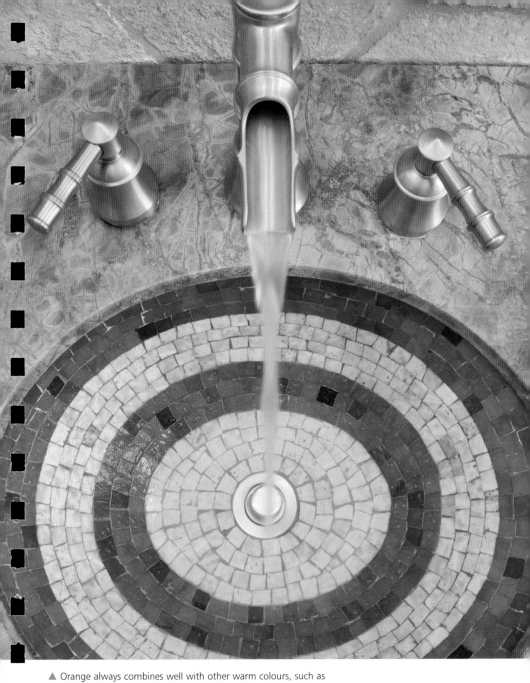

▲ Orange always combines well with other warm colours, such as
reds, and any neutrals that have a red or orange tone to them.

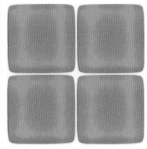

▲ **Palest peach** Orange can be the gentlest of warm colours, as shown by this soft peach tile. W

▲ **Copper** Orange glass tiles can have a coppery glow and appear to be lit from within. W

▲ **Orange mixture** Try combining light and dark versions of the same tile. W

▲ **Different versions** Take your time choosing orange-based colours as they come in many different varieties, from peach (on the left), through bold citrus orange (in the centre), to a more red-based tangerine colour (on the right). W

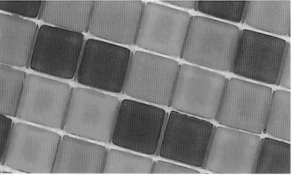

▲ **Warm floor** Linoleum tiles in warm terracotta are a more practical and safer alternative to real terracotta flooring if there are children around. F

▲ **Fruit colours** The classic colour to combine with orange is green. W

▲ **Bordered oranges** These three sets of tiling, all in slightly different shades of orange, have useful self-coloured borders and edge tiles included in the range. Orange is a colour that changes with the light, so take a range of tiles home to check the colour remains true to the one originally intended. W

▲ **Terracotta style** True terracotta has a wonderful range of colours locked within each tile, making each one unique. F

▲ **A dash of pink** A close look at this mosaic reveals a little pink has been added successfully to the blend. W

▲ **Bold linoleum** The manufacturing process of linoleum means that tiles can be manufactured in an infinite variety of effects, as these four tiles show. Patterns intensify over a large area, so try out the stronger designs in your home by buying a sample first to make sure it won't overpower the rest of the room. F

▲ **Crocodile pattern** This funky textured linoleum can be used on its own or to break up an otherwise smooth flooring surface. F

▲ **Muted orange** The typical autumn colours of muted orange and green neutrals would set off a room that catches those golden sunsets. W

▲ **Citrus zest** A set of bright orange rectangular glass tiles that would lift the spirits anywhere in the home. W

▲ **Rectangular mosaic** The colours here are an interesting mix of orange-brown with pinks and milky coffee, which would go with both terracotta flooring and cooler natural stones. W

▲ **Rich brown** When intensified, orange becomes these glowing browns. Combines well with stones. W

▲ **Embossed sprig** This leaf design on a warm peach background has a fragile appeal. W

▲ **Rough and tumble** Tumbled, irregular edges have a rural look and give an instant air of antiquity. W/F

▲ **The classic** Hand-crafted terracotta tiling is more expensive than machine made, but every tile is unique. W/F

▲ **Leaf** Like the tile above, these delicate leaf impressions demand a closer look. W

▲ **Rough and chunky** A floor paved with these tiles would give the impression of having been around for centuries. F

▲ **Lined up** Rather than use motif tiles singly, line them up in rows as shown in this splashback. W

▲ **Border motifs** Exercise caution when using picture borders with other motif tiles; ideally, they should be from the same range or they will look disjointed. W

▲ **Orange borders** Two mosaics where a warm colour has been used against a neutral background – perfect for adding to terracotta flooring patterns. F

▲ **Spiky shell** An orange-based motif tile for the bathroom as a warming alternative to popular blue. W

▲ **Fiery orange** A dazzling combination of colours will really make a picture tile stand out in the field. W

▲ **Honeysuckle** Arts and crafts designs never go out of fashion and are also available as fabrics and wallpapers, so it's possible to use a variety of textures. W

▲ **Encaustic border** A regal effect with gold set off against an opulent red-brown. F

▲ **Terracotta geometric** A hallway or conservatory with this flooring design would look sumptuous. F

▲ **Harvest plaque** This hand-painted ceramic plaque could be the centrepiece on a kitchen wall. W

▲ **Simple stripe** If you want to bring more colour into a tiled area, try a terracotta border in a straightforward design. W

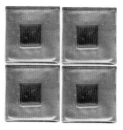

▲ **Orange insert** An unusual use of an orange centre square in an otherwise neutral glass surround. W

▲ **European leather** Vegetable-tanned cowhide tiling in a soft sand colour makes a luxurious backdrop either on walls or floors. W/F

▲ **Natural leather** One of leather's classic colours is this warm orange-brown, with the shading giving a natural variation. W/F

▲ **Tangerine border** A cheerful bathroom could be created by using tiles in this happy tangerine hue. W

▲ **Flower vase** The earthy pot in this design would pick up on any other terracotta you have in the room. W

▲ **Porcelain cream** The warmth of this cream colour means that it blends perfectly with orange-based tiling, such as terracotta. W

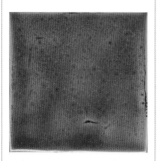

▲ **Simple ceramic** Deceptively simple, this brown-orange glaze has lots of depth and interest. W

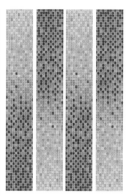

▲ **Shaded mosaic** Shaded mosaic designs can be used to grade colours up a wall or to create stripe patterns as shown. W

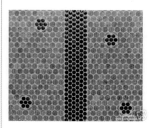

▲ **Cork mosaic** Cork tiling is naturally a rich orange-brown, and here it has been combined with a rich blue-black for an attractive contrast. W/F

▲ **Indian sandstone** Harder and more durable than limestone, sandstone is resistant to most acids, alkalis, frost and atmospheric pollution. W/F

▲ Arts and crafts wall A confident use of bold orange tiling and the honeysuckle design shown on page 89 makes for a bathroom that gets away from the conventional. W

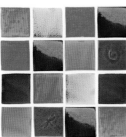

▲ Clever colours This tile design is a clever combination of red-oranges with neutrals. It would warm up a room otherwise decorated in cool colours. W

▲ Combined sizes An example of different sizes and shapes of tiles in toning colours, combined to form a strong and original overall design. W

▲ Burnt orange Cream and off-white make reliable companions to this rich burnt orange border. W

▲ **Elaborate pattern** This style of tile could be used individually among a geometric ensemble. F

▲ **Mosaic strip** Here, large-scale ceramic tiles are cleverly divided by a mosaic strip tile – an interesting alternative to the usual line of grout. F

▲ **Victorian panels** Tile panels like these were designed to be adaptable to different needs. The panel on the left could be made shorter or longer using the lower leaf tile as many times as was needed. The autumnal scene at right has an optional tile with a roundel design, here seen used both top and bottom. Five-tile panels were normal, but smaller homes could often only accommodate a three-tile panel (as at centre), for example, beside a fireplace. W

▲ **Triangle bands** Most geometric tile designs are based around the simplest of underlying tile shapes. F

▲ **Rich details** Multiple flowerheads might be too busy for normal tiles but are striking on a narrower border format. W

▲ **Strong florals** This arty border is proof that floral tiles can be bold and vivid just as easily as they can be delicate and pretty. W

▲ **Centre feature** Linoleum and vinyls can be computer-cut into bespoke designs, like this flooring centrepiece. F

▲ **Stylish fireplace** A splendid reproduction of a period fireplace, with a tiled and bordered hearth and two five-tile panels at either side, in the traditional style. The ideal was matching panels, but people in poorer homes often had to make do with a different design on either side. W

yellow

Yellow always draws the eye – it's a highly visible colour. The colour of sunshine, it will lift any cold, dark room, and pale yellows create a feeling of space. Yellow is associated with well-being and creative energy, and it is a colour of royalty, because of its similarity to gold. The welcoming colour of many spring flowers after a long winter is a pure, clear yellow; then there are the golds of autumn foliage and harvest, shading to bronzes.

yellow

Although yellow is cheerful, bright and uplifting, it can be draining if used indiscriminately over large areas. It is one of those colours that intensify when used in large amounts. What may seem like a pretty pale yellow in a single tile quickly dominates a room when used over all the walls. If a soft yellow is needed, look at the tiles in the cream colour ranges, which may appear understated at first but will often give you exactly the look you want once you have covered a large area.

Yellow's true complementary colour is violet or purple, but one of the most popular combining colours is blue, a classic combination for a country-style kitchen.

Citrus yellows, such as lemon and grapefruit, combine well with other citrus colours such as lime, tangerine and persimmon. Alternatively, you can use complementary blues and lilacs to create a softer scheme that still has some crispness to it.

Yellow fits well with its fellow warm colours – reds, terracottas and burgundies – and can give relief to an otherwise heavy scheme based on these colours.

Yellow's complementary color is purple.

▶ When yellow fades into cream it forms an excellent background colour for a warm yet calm bathroom scheme.

▲ Citrus yellow will give any room a lift – here, sculpted lemon tiles have been set among a matching field tile.

▲ **Fruit images** Food motifs are a safe choice for any kitchen and, appropriately, are said to increase appetite. W

▲ **Little bird** This popular bird motif is taken from 18th-century pottery and tile decoration. W

▲ **Diamond detail** If you don't want to cover a whole wall with a pattern, these tiles still make a good decorative border. W

▲ **Motif tiles** All kinds of images are available as motif tiles. Yellow combines perfectly with cream and other warm-based neutrals, and a room scheme based around these colours will be warm and welcoming without being overpowering. W

▲ **Tuscan travertine** Beautiful colours and a naturally pitted and banded appearance make this stone a popular choice. F

▲ **Warm or cool** Although yellow is positioned on the warm side of the colour wheel, it can be given a cooler cast by combining it with warm greys and neutrals, as on the left. Alternatively, hot it up with orange (right). W

▲ **Yellow mix** Use tiles by the same manufacturer in three or four different colours for a large-scale mosaic effect. W

▲ **Basic cream** The warmth provided by classic cream tiles means they will never go out of fashion and are always in demand. W

▲ **Warm stone** Here the warmth of the stone basins is echoed in the slightly stronger yellow tones of the mosaic behind. W

▲ **Sculpted border** This bright, uncompromising yellow will need other bright tiles to balance it. W

▲ **French yellow** Egg-yolk yellow has a touch of red in it and looks good with greys. W

▲ **Neat corner** Scatter just one or two of these tiles over a plain tiled wall. W

▲ **Cool cream** This is a cool version of cream and would go well with other beige-based neutrals. W

▲ **Soft yellow** If bright yellow doesn't appeal, try this gentler version of the colour. W

▲ **Castellation** A trim derived from classical architecture with a square-toothed design. W

▲ **Shimmering leaf** The skeleton of this leaf is only just visible on the surface of the rich glaze. W

▲ **Diamond design** Square tiles are equally effective placed on the diagonal, along with their relevant border tiles. W

▲ **Golden glaze** The beauty of this tile is in the quality of the glaze, with the yellow almost glowing. W

▲ **Kitchen motifs** Use kitchen wall tiles individually or as a frieze, as in the mouth-watering lemons on the left. W

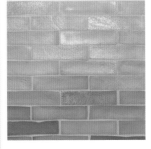

▲ **Renaissance detail** This kind of detailed tile would be used around feature fireplaces or as a horizontal band around a room. W

▲ **Silver and gold** The overall effect of this mosaic is silvery, but it includes warmer gold rectangles to balance it. W

▲ **Apricot yellow** Very warm yellow colours tend toward apricot, a useful decorating colour with none of the harshness of orange. W

▲ **Green tones** Cool yellows appear greenish, an effect intensified under artificial light. W

▲ **River panel** This tile panel combines yellow with its contrasting colour, blue. W

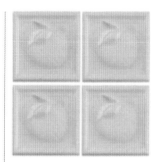

▲ **Simple sculpture** Without the addition of hand colouring, this simple sculptured fruit motif stands on its own. W

▲ **Fruit basket** A large-scale tile with yellow joined with other colours from the warm spectrum, such as orange, red and purple. W

▲ **Sculpted border** A fine tendril design pencilled over a simple border tile. W

▲ **Transfer tile** A version of the traditional transfer tile coloured in yellow hues. W

▲ **Cockerel** A design taken straight from 18th-century delftware. W

▲ **Clear yellows** If you don't want to team yellows with a contrasting colour, white is the perfect companion. W

▲ **Sunflower** A cheery motif tile in a slightly unusual rectangular format. W

▲ **Neutral yellow** Yellow can be softened with neutral tones, as in this mosaic. W

▲ **Yellow and green** Yellow can tend toward green, depending on the light. W

▲ **Putting it together** This is a classic example of late 19th- and early 20th-century amalgamation of tiles. W

▲ Quality glaze Handmade and hand decorated, the superb glaze on this tile ensures depth of colour. W

▲ Rustic An attractively rough finish is achieved by sprinkling sand onto the glaze in the final stages of production. W

▲ French glaze High-quality tiles like these are worth the added expense as they will always give a superior finish to any tiling project. W

▲ Silver lily Cream and silver may seem an unlikely pairing but, in fact, can go well together, as shown by this raised tile design. W

▲ Smudged leaf Not all motif tiles have to be bright and conspicuous – they can be a gentle contrast. W

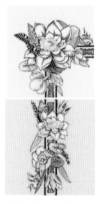

▲ Border and corner A border design with a corner tile is very versatile and enables you to make frames or outline windows and doors. W

▲ Grand statement Classical urns were a favorite Victorian style statement – here reproduced on a panel. W

▲ Stone imitation Porcelain can be manufactured to imitate stone tiles and will require less maintenance. W/F

▲ **Polished limestone** The surface of this tile has been honed to smooth it, a process that inevitably reduces the stone's natural slip-resistant properties. W

▲ **Linoleum** The return to fashion of this hard-wearing floor covering means it is now available in many attractive colours and with varied effects, such as the marbling shown in the bottom sample. F

▲ **Reproductions** A fine reproduction of a botanical drawing on tiles makes a dramatic feature when used as a centrepiece on a wall. W

▲ **High gloss** A gloss glaze suits deep yellow hues, as it makes them even more reminiscent of sunshine. W

▲ **Turning corners** It may be worth paying a little more for a range of tiles that includes a border in exactly the same colour, especially if it also includes a corner piece. W

▲ **Multipurpose tiles** The same square tile has been used on the straight and on the diagonal here. All that's needed is some practice at tile cutting. W

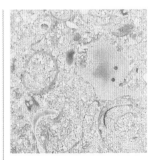

▲ **Motif medley** Here is a wonderful selection of sculpted tiles that have been hand painted. If you can't decide on one particular design, there's no reason why you shouldn't buy several of each to scatter throughout a plain tiled area. This often looks better than using only one motif throughout. W

▲ **Large-format mosaic** Slightly irregular shapes make an interesting variation on mosaic styling and mix well with streamlined interior accessories. W/F (bathroom only)

▲ **Metallic yellow** Yellow is the colour of the most precious metal, gold, which is reflected in the sheen of this mosaic. W

▲ **Limestone** Traditionally subtle in tone, the paler limestones are more porous and should be sealed well to avoid staining. W/F

Bathroom fun A perfect large tile panel for a children's bathroom – place it low enough for them to appreciate it. W

▲ **Primroses** Spring flowers will brighten up an otherwise gloomy room. W

▲ **Limestone** Natural limestone and sandstone are available in all the warm colours of the spectrum, as well as all the cool neutrals. W

▲ **Fruit border** A touch of red adds a stronger design element and widens the possibilities for accompanying colours. W

▲ **Buff mosaic** Buff yellow gives a more neutral impression than bright yellow and is a good partner with warm stones. W

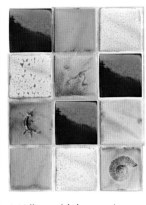

▲ **Glass-inset tile** This vibrant finish gives the effect of back-lighting, making a striking feature tile. W

▲ **Yellow with bronze** An effective combination to give an elegant touch to a yellow-based colour scheme. W

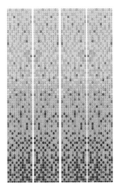

▲ **Shaded mosaic** Here a yellow mosaic has been shaded up to blues and lilacs, the complementary colours to yellow. W

▲ **Sophisticated stripes** This masculine combination of brown and yellow partners well with dark woods. W

green

Green is often seen as a difficult colour to use in decorating. It's true that when used in rooms with little natural light it does not appear at its best, but green is the archetypal colour of nature, of foliage, fields and forests, and so is perfect for bringing a verdant feel to a city flat. Muted greens are peaceful and tranquil, evoking the quietness of the countryside, whereas brighter, more vibrant greens are more stimulating – ideal for a vigorous morning wake-up in a shower or bathroom, for example.

green

Green is always refreshing to look at and restful for tired eyes. It combines perfectly with neutrals and natural materials, especially stones.

Lighter greens tending toward blue are serene and elegant and often used to create a cool, 18th-century feel.

Dark jungle greens can appear rich and mysterious, and they look good combined with the sparkle of glass and the sheen of chrome or other metallic finishes. Clear, fresh white is another partner for dark green, giving it a lift away from institutional cream and green, which can often look dated.

Green can be used as a link between a garden and living spaces, such as conservatories. This doesn't have to be a big statement: just a simple green accent tile in terracotta flooring will form a link between inside and outside, and tie in with any indoor planting.

Green and red were a popular Victorian combination but can be uncomfortable, as the colours are so highly contrasting. Done with verve, this combination is still very effective in a room that is not in continuous use – a period-style bathroom, for example. However, using an alternative to red, still in the warm spectrum, such as terracotta or coral, makes a more acceptable scheme for a kitchen used throughout the day.

Green's complementary colour is red.

▲ Aqua is a colour in the green spectrum and can be offset by using white and other neutrals as a contrast.

▲ Both bath and shower have been cleverly combined here,
with the whole area covered in a spring green mosaic tile.

▲ **Soft apple** A fresh green combines well with white and looks best with clean white grout lines. W

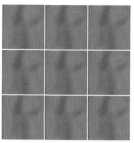

▲ **Jade green** This green is verging on the blue and makes a good mix with other blue-based colours, including navy. W

▲ **Oriental simplicity** A very modern look can be created using a rectangular tile in a plain colour, such as this celadon green. F

▲ **Useful trims** Matching trims, particularly when they include corners, create a neat finish to tile areas that end halfway up a wall. They can also be used to make frames for tile picture panels. W

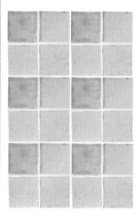

▲ **Green and natural** Green mixes perfectly with all the natural tones. W

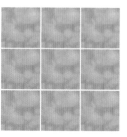

▲ **Summer zing** This combination of colours brings the fresh summer outdoors into the home. W

▲ **Marble effect** Deep natural colours with polished surfaces can be a source of light reflection in the room, even if they are dark hues. F

▲ **Natural stone effect** These glazed porcelain tiles have a soft, smooth finish and riven edges to enhance their overall aesthetic. Suitable for some outdoor areas. F

▲ **Border tile** A coordinating edge tile finishes off an area, and a toning grout achieves a designer look. W

▲ **Leaf green glass** Lime greens look best combined with other citrus colours, such as lemon yellow and tangerine. W

▲ **Hexagon** An unusually shaped tile like this honeycomb pattern needs to be laid accurately to look good. W/F

▲ **Green combination** Many different tile sizes and shapes within a simple palette of green-coloured glass have been used here to great effect, including the almost invisible glass shelf. W

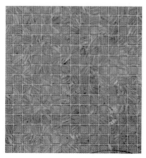 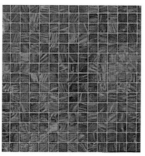

▲ **Olive green** This version of green is not commonly found in tiles but combines beautifully with terracotta. W

▲ **Green mosaics** Some fine examples of green colours combined with neutrals for a relaxed, natural look. These would give a restful air to a bathroom and could be used with stone or neutral flooring. W

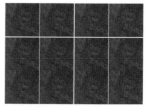

▲ **Jade glass** This jade green is an alternative to the classic turquoise for bathrooms, and it gives an oriental feel. W

▲ **Summer stripes** These would be perfect for a feature wall, as the individual tiles build up into a striking set of graduated stripes. W

▲ **Background green** Tiles are perfect for providing a textured background in a beautiful colour without dominating the room. W

 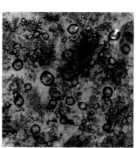

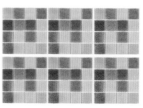

▲ **Rich texture** An unusual combination of green with its complementary pink-red and a velvety black. W

▲ **Naturals** Adding green to blue, such as in this mosaic, gives a countryside feel that would link in with the colours of the garden outside. W

▲ **Plain green glass** This light, spring green tile would freshen up any area, particularly one that is poorly lit. W

▲ **Blue reflections** Such an expanse of mosaic tiling illustrates just how amazing it can look. Other decorative accessories can be kept to a minimum for a winning Zen-inspired aesthetic that's crisp and clean. W

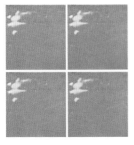

▲ **Lustre** Pearlescent finishes retain simplicity of colour whilst adding a hint of sparkle, which would add an individual touch to a contemporary kitchen. W

▲ **Green-blue floor** Linoleum tiles have a random pattern that builds up to create a softly textured floor. F

▲ **Peacock tiles** Peacock blues and greens are glowing colours that go well with black as a contrast colour. W

▲ **Tile bands** Mosaic and other small-format tiles don't have to be used all over a wall. They can be inserted as bands where the main area is decorated with less expensive field tiles. These inserts can be quite narrow, yet still give the impression of attention to detail in the room scheme, making them a sound investment for the budget-conscious home decorator. W

▲ **Flower power** Because mosaics are so versatile, a decorative panel can be any size you like – or any size you need to fill a specific space. W

▲ **Versatile vert** These five versions of linoleum tiles show just how varied green can be, and how well it combines with other colours. The samples here range from a grey-green for minimalist interiors, through a rich brown-olive, to greens combined with orange for a look that's similar to exotic marble. There's a green that will go in almost any interior, whether you want it to be understated or the focus of the room. F

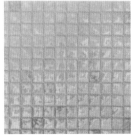

▲ **Glass beads** A very tactile tile made using tiny glass balls set into the surface. W

▲ **Light or bright** Green mosaics can form a subtle background in almost neutral shades (left), or they can be the centre of attention in uplifting colours (right). W

▲ Metropolitan style The subway-tile shape has a chic, urban air. W

▲ Classic colours This green and blue combination of glass mosaic is a classic for bathrooms and a dependable choice. W

▲ Moody blues This mosaic could appear to be either blue or green depending on the light. Both black and white go well with it. W

▲ Seashell A graceful mosaic with a delicate shell-like finish. W

▲ Opaque green-blue An opaque finish to a mosaic is just as effective as the translucency of glass. These two closely matching colours could be used on opposite walls in a bathroom. W

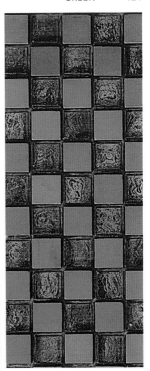

▲ **Ceramic tile combinations** Standard ceramic tiles can be combined on a wall in the same way ready-made mosaic tiles are combined, in toning or contrasting colours. Take time with a few tiles to create your perfect colour combination before buying enough to decorate the whole room. W

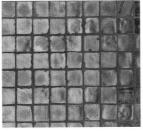

▲ **Total transparency** When laying clear white glass tiles, such as the ones shown here in combination with darker ones, avoid all bubbles in the adhesive below. W

▲ **Iridescent glass** Some high-end hand-finished mosaics are also suitable for use on bathroom floors. W/F

▲ **Natural elements** Even a modern finish can be reminiscent of the natural environment, which provides useful inspiration to the home decorator. W

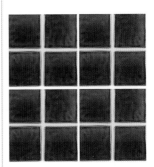

▲ **Water inspired** The prevailing theme of water in these reflective tiles makes them perfect for the bathroom. W

▲ **Glamorous mosaics** If the beauty of these mosaics appeals, try using them in wide horizontal bands around the room or as a splashback behind a shelf with simpler tiling above and below. W

▲ **High-gloss field tiles** Glazed edges on this type of tile ensure a professional finish to large areas of tiling. W

▲ **Dado tile** For a touch of calm elegance, a simple dado shape in a creamy green is hard to beat. W

▲ **Leaf mosaic** Mosaic artists use different sizes of mosaic pieces to create their bold designs. W

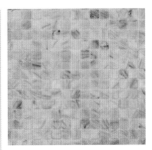

▲ **Textured glass** Completely handmade, this modern high-end glass tile is especially lustrous when highlighted by subtle illumination, such as candlelight. W

▲ **Metallic green** You could pick up on the yellow-green reflections here for the rest of the room scheme. W

▲ **Basically natural** If you didn't want to emphasize the green, this mosaic has just a hint of it in a natural background. W/F (bathroom only)

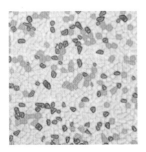

▲ **Speckled glass** Purple and green speckle the surface of this otherwise almost transparent glass tile. W/F (bathroom only)

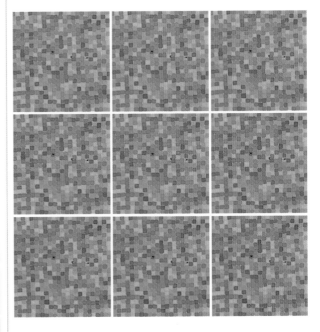

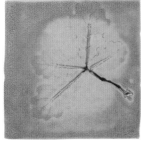

▲ **Cotton ball** Many motif tiles have a basic white or cream background; this one has green, so could be placed in a green or cream tile background. W

▲ **Irregular shapes** Achieve contrived, highly original designs with intriguing curves and richly contrasting colours. W/F (bathroom only)

▲ **Bubbles** A perfect theme for a bathroom – note how the tiles have been used both as a continuous panel and singly, scattered on the opposite wall among the classic white tiles. W

▲ **Glass mosaic** Mixed hues in this large-format mosaic tile will reflect soft yellows and natural tones. W

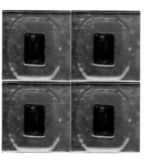

▲ **Designer glass** The designer has produced a jewel-like effect here, setting the glass in the more muted background. W

▲ **Waves** This is a tube-lined design, where the colours are skilfully filled in by hand. W

Sculpted tiles All of these sculpted wall tiles are hand painted, making each one individual. The turtle and frog would make excellent inserts in a plain bathroom scheme. The olive band would fit perfectly in a Mediterranean-style kitchen, used on its own or combined with other tiles with a Mediterranean theme. The floral wreath would be perfect in a country-style kitchen with plants and flowers part of the décor. W

▲ **Arts and crafts** This tile is inspired by the designs of the arts and crafts movement, with animals and plants intricately twined together. W

▲ **Country leaves** A continuous leaf border is always appealing – this one has a useful and stylish corner tile included. W

▲ **Pond masterpiece**
A large sculpted tile that
shows off the expertise of
the tile painter. W

▲ **Mixed genres** These tiles artfully fuse together
traditional motifs that have been used in home
décor for centuries but with a more modern fiery-
orange background. W

Green motif tiles Motif tiles may seem expensive, but you only need a few of them to create a really distinctive room scheme. Place them anywhere among plainer tiles, but keep most of them at around eye level or lower for full appreciation. A mixture of several tile designs looks more imaginative than if you use only one. Most manufacturers supply a plain field tile that is exactly the same as the background of the motif tile so they blend seamlessly. However, you can mix and match from several manufacturers if you prefer, but do check that the background colours of the tiles go well together. There is a danger that warmer creams can make cooler cream colours look dull and dingy. W

▲ **Tree panel** Twelve tiles make up this individually crafted large-format panel with a botanical theme. W

Harvest festival A cornucopia of fruits and vegetables is perfect for a country kitchen and complements furniture in mid-toned woods, such as pine and oak. Alternatively, they would look good in a painted kitchen – plain white or cream – or one in which the colours in the tiles are picked up in the painting. These tiles should not be surrounded by too many competing colours, so keep painted walls and the ceiling fairly neutral. Accessorize the kitchen with real fruit and flowers. Terracotta flooring would complete the look. W

▲ **Encaustic tile** Top-class handmade tiles like this require care when being installed for optimum finish. Always check sealing instructions too. W/F

▲ **Geometric band** Regency colours are ideal for use in period properties. W/F

▲ **Green abstract** This narrow insert tile is designed to make bands of abstract colour through a field of plain tiling. W

▲ **On the diagonal** A clever use of rectangular tiles in a diagonal format will involve some expert tile cutting. W

▲ **Wallpaper effect** Covering large areas or entire walls in these tiles would create the effect of a late 19th-century wallpaper. W

▲ **Cool geometrics** Here geometric tiles in cool colours have been combined with classic buff to make flooring patterns that are lighter and fresher than those including reds and terracottas. Note how an almost three-dimensional effect can be created using light and dark alternately (at the top of the left-hand panel). F

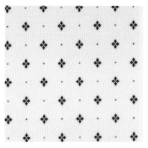

▲ **Four-leaf clover** These tiles give a wallpaper effect but with the toughness of a glazed finish. W

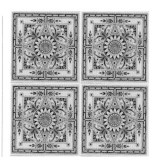

▲ **Victorian single tiles** These beautiful period floral tiles can be used as highlights in a plain field or grouped together as a large frieze. W

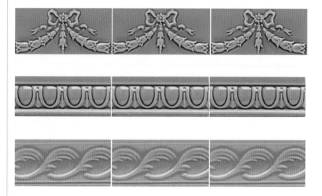

▲ **Green border tiles** It's worth considering a range of tiles that include borders and edge tiles like these for the professional finish it will give to your tiling. You will find that they will add texture and interest to the room, avoiding the need to resort to elaborate colour schemes. Although dado height is the conventional position, many of them look good placed higher up – the swag design (top), for example, would be perfect for this. W

▲ **Rococo scene** Copying classical painting styles onto tiles was all the fashion in the 19th century. W

▲ **Seaweed and fish** A very artistic design in muted colours. W

Tile style This is how patterned tiles were traditionally combined with contrasting deep colours to cover a whole room. This uncompromising approach is extremely effective if done with confidence and gives you an opportunity to use all aspects of the tile manufacturer's art, including mouldings and borders. The tiles at left are other typical examples of possible bold combinations. Make sure you have a substantial area of plain tiling to set off all the different patterns. W

▲ **Heraldic design** Repeat this hand-painted design across an entire wall area, or use to form drop-in panels. W

▲ **American glazed** These octagonal tiles are combined with insets and bordered with top-cap moulding in rich green. W

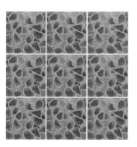

▲ **Recycled glass** Eco-friendly recycled glass produces these beautiful textures and patterns in the surface. W

▲ **Matt glaze** A matt finish and a similar design makes these tiles fit together in a perfect ensemble. W/F

▲ **Irregular mosaic** Mosaic tiles don't have to be of a regular pattern. This more random design would break up a large wall area. W

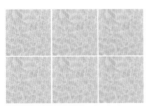

▲ **Marble effect in glass** Recycled glass gives a range of surface effects, including this delicate marbled green. W

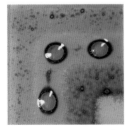

▲ **Contemporary motif** These green and blue tiles build up into a contemporary design reminiscent of traditional Victorian tiles. W

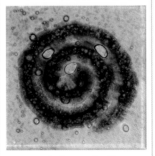

▲ **Fun spirals** Use tiles like these as accent tiles or in a band around a bath or above a sink. W

▲ **Framed** Bold colours and a brilliant jade-green frame make these modern tube-lined tiles really sparkle. W

blue

Blue is said to be most people's favourite colour, but like green, it needs to be chosen with care when used for decorating. The colour of peace and harmony, blue also conveys intellectual endeavour. For this reason, it is frequently used by companies and institutions – often combined with whites and greys – for office interiors and company logos. Blue is too useful a colour to be left in the office, and it is perfect for creating a specific mood in the home.

blue

Delft and Wedgewood blues are typical of the 16th and 17th centuries, when the classic delft tiling was the height of fashion. Combined with white and off-whites, these blues still make an excellent bathroom or kitchen scheme.

Strong turquoises and sky blues with a terracotta floor suggest the warmth of a Mediterranean summer. Lighten these blues with a cooler-coloured stone floor, and you have a more laid-back West Coast style.

Blue has a low light-reflectance value, so it tends to soften strong light. It can therefore be used to calm an overbright room. Light blues appear to expand a space, whereas the deeper tones — which suggest the night sky or the depth of the ocean — are more enclosing. Very bold, intense blues, such as cobalt, can be overpowering, so reserve them for accents and accessories.

Blues combine well with wood tones and with metallics like silver and pewter.

Due to its association with cleanness and freshness, blue is without a doubt the first choice for swimming pool tiles, offering some coolness on a hot summer's day. Even in winter, a blue or turquoise pool can lift the spirits and remind you of a summer sky.

Blue's complementary colour is orange.

▶ Blue staircase tiles look good against their complementary colour, orange, which is featured in the terracotta tiling of the treads.

▲ Brilliant cobalt blue is always a winner for a bathroom
or shower area, and all it needs with it is pure white, and
perhaps a touch of natural wood.

▲ **Sky blue** This gentle blue will never be overpowering. W

▲ **Warm blue** Blues with a touch of red in them give a warmer feel for a north-facing interior. W

▲ **Soft effect** The yellow tones in this mosaic could be used to decorate the rest of the room. W

▲ **Delft tile** A classic delft design with the characteristic corner motifs. W

▲ **Pink combination** Pink and blue in a very pretty mosaic mixture. W

▲ **Fruit sculpture** A typical delft-style motif given the sculpted treatment for greater impact. W

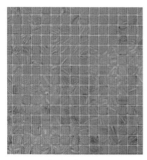

▲ **Warm blue** A tropical shade of blue takes away the potential coldness the colour is capable of projecting. W

▲ **Textured surface** Apart from adding interest, a textured surface, such as this diamond-patterned one, will aid grip when used as flooring. W/F

▲ **Veining** Subtle lines give the appearance of natural stones like marble. F

▲ **Turquoise haven** Lighter blues mix perfectly with contemporary chrome bathroom fittings. W

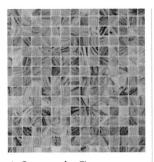

▲ **Grey combo** The greys mingle well in this mosaic while permitting the blue to retain its depth. W

▲ **Fossil leaf** This leaf skeleton has an ageless quality about it. Combine with white or with a carefully chosen plain blue tile. W

▲ **Almost purple** Cobalt blue always makes an impact and has an appealing richness. W

▲ **Varying size** Using different widths of tile in a border is highly effective and helps break up a large area of tiles in a regular pattern. W

▲ **Blue slip** Insert a slim border like this into an area of inexpensive white or cream tiling for instant class. W

▲ **Linoleum tile** An advantage of modern linoleum is that it makes a whole range of unusual colours available for flooring. F

▲ **Quality glaze** Blue is one of the most deserving colours to have its depth brought out by a high-end glaze. W

▲ **Sea blue** The depth of colour here is stunning – use sparingly as a splashback or border. W

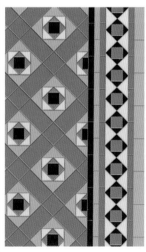

▲ **Geometric style** A more modern colourway for a geometric floor using blue and its complementary colour, yellow. F

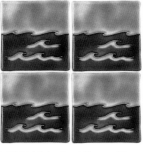

▲ **Nautical theme** Decorative hand-painted tube-lined tiles could be used singly or together in a bathroom accessorized in blue and white to keep with the nautical theme. Natural rope is also a complementary design addition. W

▲ **Botanical** Naturalistic plant designs are always easy on the eye and go well just about anywhere. W

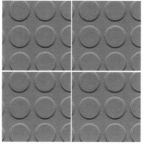

▲ **Daisy** Traditionally, this type of tile would be used in a band around a hallway, kitchen or porch. W

▲ **Rubber** Flooring made of this slip-resistant material comes in lots of colours and tones nowadays, including this soft blue. F

▲ **Islamic inspiration** This tile builds up into a complex overall design reminiscent of the decoration of palaces. W

▲ **Lavender** Combine gentle lavender blue with lime greens and whites. W

▲ **Fern** If you can't find a match to the background colour of a motif tile like this, use white or cream for the field tile. W

▲ **Contrast** This mosaic contrasts a highly textured surface with a very plain one in a chequered effect. W

▲ **Sophisticated duck egg** This classy hue is as equally suited to a country house as it is a city flat. W

▲ **English delft** Hand-decorated recreations of originals can look as good as the real thing. W

▲ **Skilful combination** Blues and whites make an excellent combination, especially when different sizes and textures are also used. W

▲ **Touch of blue** White tiles that have a touch of blue are useful to mix with any of the stronger blues. W

▲ **Turquoise sheen** The surface of this tile changes colour depending on the way you look at it – a well-lit room will unleash its full potential. W

▲ **Grey-blue encaustic** A blue that is bordering on grey makes a natural partner for white or cream. F

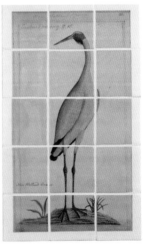

▲ **Bird panel** A large wall panel with an elegant bird design that could be used instead of, or combined with, more usual botanical tile panels. W

▲ **English clay** An uneven surface texture enables the glaze to pool, thus adding interest to the overall look. W

▲ **Rubber flooring** Rubber floor tiles are given non-slip properties with this ridged surface pattern. F

▲ **Satin finish** Minimal application of glaze and gloss can also be attractive, as this handmade stone-effect tile shows. W

▲ **Jewel squares** These tiles could be rotated during laying to give a random arrangement to the coloured squares. W

▲ **Marble effect** Over a large surface area, the colours in this patterned linoleum will blend into an overall natural-looking effect. F

▲ **Lilac sheen** Tiles with a beautiful lustre finish can be combined with similar tiles in matching colours. W

▲ **Linoleum flooring** These modern linoleum tiles demonstrate how versatile blue can be. As a cool colour, it is often combined with warmer pinky-purples and warm neutrals to keep it from looking too cold, as in the tiles left and centre. The tile on the right is a dramatic purple-blue and black, which could be highly effective in a small room, such as a study. F

▲ **Convolvulus** There's a touch of yellow in this sculpted and hand-painted tile, which you could draw from to accessorize the room. W

▲ **Blue bands** Thin bands of beautiful colour can be set into plainer tiles. W

▲ **Using motif tiles** This motif tile has been cleverly matched to the blue of the surrounding field tile. Note the use of a natural-coloured grout, which suits the tiles far better than white would have done. W

▲ **Natural panel** The natural theme of this large wall panel is carried out in a mixture of soft neutral tones. W

▲ **Simple glass** Put this band of small alternating blue glass squares between lines of larger tiles. W

▲ **Herb motif** Culinary herbs are an obvious choice to decorate a rustic kitchen. W

▲ **Turkish tulip** The tulip motif and strong shades of turquoise are highly characteristic of oriental decoration. W

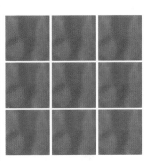

▲ **Cornflower** This shade of blue is attractive on its own as a field of tiles, or it could be combined with natural creams and greens. W

▲ **Reflections** Highly reflective tiles give a sense of life and movement as the light changes. W

▲ **Victorian floral** Match the buttermilk of the background with a plain contrasting tile. W

▲ **Netted design** A complex eastern tile design that would look good as a panel with a rich blue edging. W

▲ **Muted delft** This tile uses a typical 18th-century tile design but in a softer blue than usual. W

▲ **Mixed mosaic** An ensemble that mixes every blue from ice cool to dark cobalt. W

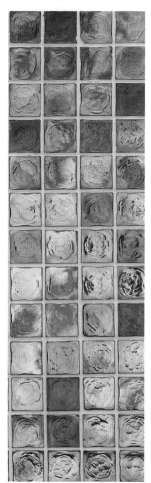

▲ **Solo performance** Use a simple background of greys and blues in a mosaic of this beauty and complexity. W

▲ **Blue border** This sculpted tile border would go with any other classic blue and white tiles. W

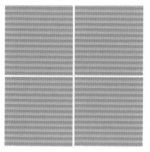

▲ **Rubber** With its anti-slip, anti-static and noise-absorbing properties, rubber can be a wise choice of floor tile. F

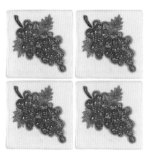

▲ **Grape motif** Deep blue-purples are a sound choice for pine and oak wood kitchens. W

▲ **Tile contrast** A classic complementary combination of blues with their opposites on the colour wheel — yellows and oranges. W

▲ **Sapphire** This band with bright sapphire blue in it would be all you need to lift an all-white bathroom. W

▲ **Garden greens** A geometric encaustic border suitable for a conservatory or greenhouse as it would combine well with foliage green. F

▲ **Lighter touch** Incorporating blue with contrasting warm neutral colours has stunning results. F

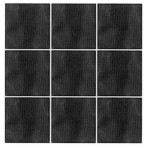

▲ **Blue field** A simple strong blue tile acts as a foil for lighter motif tiling. W

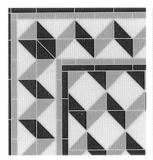

▲ **Tumbling blocks** This pattern gives a clever three-dimensional effect in a mix of refined colours. F

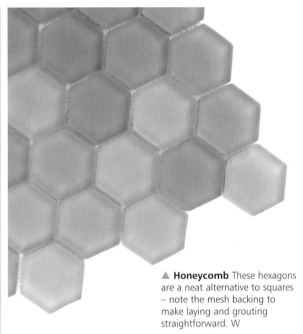

▲ **Honeycomb** These hexagons are a neat alternative to squares – note the mesh backing to make laying and grouting straightforward. W

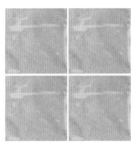

▲ **Watery finish** There's an almost liquid effect to the surface of these tiles. W

▲ **Dark jade** A bold colour that could be used with both black and white very successfully. W

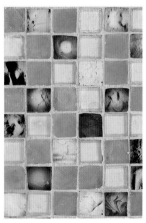

▲ **Fine detail** Every square in this mosaic appears slightly different, giving a hand-crafted effect. W

▲ **Sultry slate** The darkest of the stone finishes, with a rough, riven finish. F

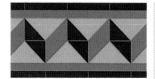

▲ **Zigzag** Building up complex patterns is easy with geometric tiles. F

▲ **Turn of the century** Early 20th-century designs typically had these sinuous natural shapes. W

▲ **Uncompromising** Add masses of impact with this purple tiling with strong blue detailing. W

▲ **Masterpiece** Make a big style statement with classical art transferred to ceramic panels. W

▲ **Transfer tile** Victorian transfer tiles were hand coloured, here in a soft gentian blue. W

▲ **William Morris** This pattern is typical of the 19th-century British wallpaper and fabric designer. W

▲ **Delft motif** A delicate centre flower tile, similar to delft designs but without the corner motifs. W

▲ **Butterfly** British Victorian fireplaces were often decorated with extravagant flower and insect designs like this one. W

▲ **Texture detail** Mosaic squares have been used in three different versions for a most effective bathroom scheme. W

▲ **Art nouveau** Here, natural forms have become highly stylized – use this tile repeated to form a horizontal border. W

▲ **Morris flower** The late 19th-century arts and crafts designs are perennial favorites. W

▲ **Leaf border** A good border for a bathroom, either as an insert or to top an area of tiling. W

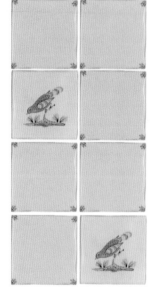

▲ **Delft bird** Delft tiling was always mix and match, with plainer tiles often alternating with more expensive motif tiles. W

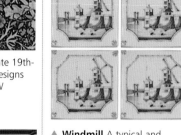

▲ **Windmill** A typical and popular Dutch scene for a kitchen or fire surround. W

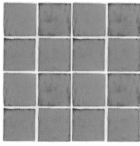

▲ **Fashionable turquoise** This attractive colour has recently enjoyed a surge in popularity. W

▲ **Multiples** When covering a smaller area with the same tile, be sure to check any stipulations on minimum orders. W

▲ **Flower vase** This tall tile panel with a flower vase theme would have been very popular in the 19th century for stove surrounds or in hallways. W

▲ **Bow and swag** The swag design is a classic and has been used for centuries. W

▲ **Repeating design** Several border tiles will need to be put together to gauge the full impact of the design. W

▲ **Deco tiles** Designs from the art deco movement were based on geometric shapes, plain colours and bold contrasts. W

▲ **Flowerhead** A contemporary version of the flower tile. W

▲ **Three blues** A medley of three closely related hues from the same tile manufacturer can be very striking. W

▲ **Blueberry** A border to bring just a touch of blue to a scheme based around cream. W

▲ **Glass flower** A flower effect has been inserted into this glass mosaic by using different coloured glass pieces. W

▲ **Splash** Two strong blues make a powerful and dynamic design statement. W

▲ **Contemporary glass** This dark blue designer glass tile has green overtones. W

▲ **Flower panel** There's enough blue in this tile panel for it to be placed in a blue-based room scheme, though the rich reds could be brought out too. W

▲ **Prestigious florals** Reflect the natural beauty of the garden with intertwined floral designs. W

▲ **Sleeping maiden** Elegant women adorn many tall panel designs. W

▲ **Graded glass** A narrow slip of rich rainbow glass can be inserted into a bed of bigger tiles. W

▲ **Blue stud** Bold tile studding contrasts well with a smooth tile surface. W

▲ **Flare** This tile design has the effect of a flash of blue flame. W

▲ **Blue iris** Tall flowers in a vase are useful when you want to create the illusion of height in a room. W

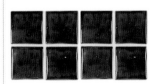

▲ **Cool Gothic** Gothic tracery is given a contemporary twist with this flooring design in sage green and fine pewter blue. F

▲ **Stone and mosaic** The mosaic band here has been finished off with bands of stone that match the stone tiling beneath. W

▲ **Steel blue** Very dark navy blues become steely in tone and blend well with silver-coloured metals in the rest of the room. W

▲ **Plain glass** These handmade glass tiles come in a complete spectrum of colours. W

▲ **Crackle-glazed terracotta** With these crackle-glazed terracotta tiles and their distressed edges you can create your own history. W/F

▲ **Moulded, glazed border and field** This traditional configuration of deep moulding, border and chequered field tiles would look wonderful anywhere in a period home. W

▲ **Mixing designs** Glazed, printed decoration on unglazed floor tiles. Don't put the décors in high-traffic areas. F

▲ **Classical** For a classical scheme, choose these timeless embossed-motif glazed wall tiles. W

▲ **Decorated glass** Glass tiles are particularly effective in shades of blue and team well with plain white tiles. W

▲ **Hand glazed** These handmade, hand-glazed tiles have a natural variation of colour that makes the whole wall positively glow. W

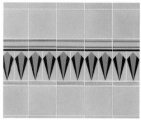

▲ **Art-deco-style ceramic** This panel is a faithful modern copy of the original art deco tiles. W

▲ **Wide range** A selection of blue borders, listellos and mouldings. W

▲ **Spanish glazed floor tiles**
These traditional glazed floor tiles can be used around the outside of a room or in the middle to look like a rug. F

▲ **Delft-effect glazed wall**
These glazed tiles would look perfect in a country kitchen or small tearoom. W

▲ **Water-jet cut motif** This is a water-jet cut panel. You can have your own design, company logo or family crest. W

▲ **Glass mosaic wall**
Glass mosaic with a pale blue waterproof grout. Ideal for a wetroom. W

▲ **Victorian reproduction**
Faithfully reproduced Victorian wall tiles can be used as fire surrounds and tabletops. W

▲ **Matt-glazed clay** These tiles could be used to form a distinctive chequered pattern with plain coordinating field tiles or as borders or panels. W

▲ **Combining tiles** Two typical panel layouts in blue glazed wall tiles. W

▲ **Relief wall tiles** Choose your theme: boats, animals, fruit or village scenes. W

▲ **Colour-changing glass** These glass wall tiles actually change colour as you walk past them. W

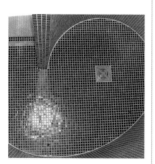

▲ **Bathroom blues** Blue mosaic floor and wall tiles in a snail shower. No door, no curtain, no fuss. W/F

▲ **Natural stone** Slate and natural stone floor tiles are hard to find in a true blue. They are usually found with variegated earth tones against grey-blue, as with those shown above. F

▲ **Colour combinations** Don't be afraid to team blue with its exact opposite. The result can be surprisingly soft and easy on the eye. W

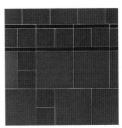

▲ **Porcelain floor tiles**
Different sizes of plain blue tiles fixed in an imaginative way are very effective. F

▲ **Hand-painted brights** Use such boldly patterned tiles carefully in small spaces or where tiles may need to be cut awkwardly, as this could disrupt the symmetry of the overall pattern. W

▲ **Faux handmade glaze**
These 10 x 10 cm (4 x 4 in.) tiles have a machine-applied glaze that makes them look handmade. They would look great in a country-themed home or used to add a glow to a contemporary kitchen. W

▲ **Glass mosaic border** Stylish but inexpensive, a glass mosaic border can be set in plain white wall tiles. Try vertical borders to create stripes and panels. W

▲ **Liquid effect** The bubbles in this glass tile give the illusion of water, a perfect theme for the bathroom. W

▲ **Fleur-de-lis set** This delightful fleur-de-lis taco and border set would look perfect with blue or white tiles. W

▲ **Hand glazed** It's easy to tell from the texture and glaze variation that this wall tile is hand glazed. W

neutrals

In decorating, neutrals are taken to mean the colours associated with natural fibres, such as linen, cotton and calico, and natural stone and wood. They are softer and easier to use than pure black and white. They can be used on their own or as a background to richer colours and are often used as a background field tile with accents in a stronger colour.

neutrals

Neutrals are wide ranging and include beige, off-white, taupe, mushroom and magnolia. Easy to live with, they can appear bland and a little over-safe unless given some accents or texture as a contrast. However, there's no doubt they make for harmonious and restful interiors: a soft and tranquil background by day; more glowing and warm by artificial light at night.

Although neutrals are very accommodating, it's not true they all go with one another. All beiges are not the same! You will find they tend to fall into two camps – yellow-based neutrals and pink-based neutrals – and the two are not always successful when put side by side. This is why beautiful stone can seem inviting in the showroom, but dull and almost dirty when placed into a room with colours that do not bring out its natural qualities. Always check a neutral colour in situ, particularly one used over a large area, to avoid disappointment. For similar reasons, tinted whites and off-whites need careful colour matching to make an effective scheme.

Neutral schemes benefit from using lots of textural contrast to provide interest. This means combining different surface finishes – shiny, silky, matt, rough, shaggy – and small and large patterns on the surfaces. The natural variations in marbles, stones, granites and their imitations come into use here. Against these, fabrics add another dimension – from chunky, fluffy towels, to light-filtering sheers and voiles.

▶ Neutrals dominate this airy dining room, with dark woods contrasting with the pale sheen of the tiled floor.

▲ Grey and cream might not seem an obvious combination,
but the touch of grey in this bathroom gives definition.

▲ **Pink and grey** Neutral combinations based on grey are warmed by the addition of pink. W

▲ **Earth tones** This large-format natural-looking floor tile is perfect for a masculine bathroom with dark wood fittings. F

▲ **Diamond** Very simple border designs like this can have a big impact once they are repeated around a room. W

▲ **Green window** This ultra-modern tile has green glass inserts – use to create a border or frame effect. W

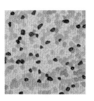

▲ **Bold** A confident mix of texture and colour, as with this pebble-dashed effect, is stunning on the right surfaces. W

▲ **Raised fruit** Use same-coloured sculpted tiles where you want to add texture but not extra colour. W

▲ **Off-white** Hints of many different colours can be picked up in marbled off-whites, such as the green and blue apparent here. F

▲ **Classic marble** Grey marble usually has some warm brown or beige veining if you look closely. W/F

▲ **Touch of tangerine** Orange shades to a neutral background will go well with terracotta flooring. W

▲ **Warm neutrals** Cool taupe grey has been combined with warmer neutrals in this mosaic. W/F

▲ **Light-catching stone** Natural-looking stone doesn't need a glaze to be reflective – its smooth surface will do the trick. W

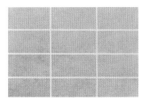

▲ **Rectangular blocks** A very modern look is created by using tiles with the emphasis on the horizontal. W

▲ **Chef's kitchen** Garlic bulbs and other food-related motifs should be included in the décor of any keen cook's kitchen. W

▲ **Mosaic mixture** A glittering floor including glass ovals can be set off by plain white furniture. W/F

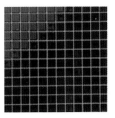

▲ **Glowing chestnut** This dark nut brown would contrast with any warm stone colours. W/F

▲ **Matt and modern** This brown mosaic is almost black, with an attractive metallic finish. Find a dark grout to match it. W/F

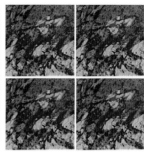

▲ **Infusions** Here natural stone and brown marble have been combined to maximize the pattern. W

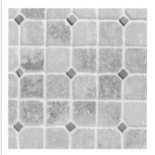

▲ **Inserts** Insert tiles can be as simple as these small diamonds and still break up a large tiled area successfully. F

▲ **Square mosaic** These ready-made mosaic panels are perfect for the corners of a terracotta floor. F

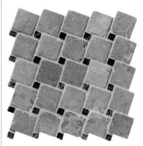

▲ **Crossways** It would be difficult to lay this mosaic design using individual units, but this is a mesh-backed tile for instant results. W/F

▲ **Linoleum floor** A hard-wearing floor surface in a warm neutral colourway is ideal for high-traffic areas in the home, such as hallways. F

▲ **The natural world** The unusual bark pattern on this tile opens up exciting possibilities for incorporating elements of nature into the décor. F

▲ **Café au lait** A soft brown hue would never be over-powering. W

▲ **Striking stone** This is an impressive example of the vivid colour combinations that can be found in some stone tiles. F

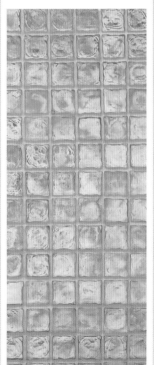

▲ **Geometric neutrals** Coffee and butterscotch colours combine well with just a touch of dark green in this geometric floor. F

▲ **Dusky pink** This light rose hue has subtle cream undertones. W

▲ **Glass neutrals** Glass tiles create their own version of neutrals, like this gently coloured mosaic. W

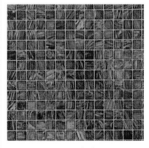

▲ **Green neutral** The green-based neutrals here are given added dimension by the flash of peach behind them. W

▲ **Minimalist style** Plain porcelain tiling on the left
contrasts with a wall of basket-weave mosaic, all in
minimalist neutrals offset with black and white towels. W

▲ **Chunky cream** Good-quality cream tiling will always appeal as a field tile. W

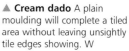

▲ **Cream dado** A plain moulding will complete a tiled area without leaving unsightly tile edges showing. W

▲ **Grey slate** There is colour and detail even in simple slate when you look closely. F

▲ **Creamy white** The uneven quality of the glaze surface of this tile is part of its charm. W

▲ **Tuscan travertine** The worn finish on some natural stone tiles makes them a pleasure to walk on barefooted – an experience best suited to those in warmer climates! F

▲ **Square cut** The sides of these mosaic squares are clean-cut edges to give a smart finish to the tiling. W/F

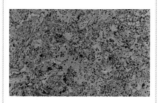

▲ **Softer flooring** Natural cork provides warmth, noise insulation and a soft surface upon which to tread. F

▲ **Tumbled surface** Some stone mosaics have deliberately softened edges and surfaces. W/F

▲ **Building patterns** This arrangement shows how patterns can be built up using neutral, natural stone. W

▲ **Subtle stone** Simple stones like this give an air of glamorous luxury when used throughout a bathroom. W/F

▲ **Coffee twist** Add this border to an area of matching tiles, or use as a contrast with white. W

▲ **Squared-off stones** A pink-based neutral stone ensemble, to be mixed with any of the terracotta tiles that also tend toward pink. W/F

▲ **Graded colour** The colours in this mosaic grade from muted greens to neutrals. W

▲ **Dark leaves** A dark fir green is a less common neutral tone, but is very effective when combined with terracotta. F

▲ **Basket weave** Use a detailed stone arrangement like this in bands or panels with a toning plain stone tile. W

▲ **Greek scroll** This wave design has been used in decoration for thousands of years and is still a classic. W

▲ **Coffee and cream** A tried and tested colour combination with square tiles used diagonally in the centre for an individual touch. W

▲ **Coloured cork** Perhaps surprisingly, due to its pink overtones, this tile is natural cork. F

▲ **Neutral mix** Many versions of neutral work well together in a mixture of light and dark. W

▲ **Roman floor** If you want to copy the grandeur of ancient Rome, then use a ready-made mosaic panel like this one. F

▲ **Earth-toned walls** Go against the norm and use dark-coloured naturals on walls as well as floors. W/F

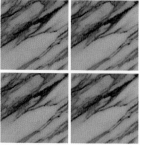

▲ **Bold veins** The veining in stones can be prominent, and care must be taken in the placing and orientation of each tile. W/F

▲ **Tree bark** A highly textured surface can't be used for work surfaces but is very successful on walls. W

▲ **Pitted stone** In contrast to the shine of highly glazed tiles, some are left with a deliberately rough finish. W/F

▲ **Glass roundels** Multihued glass roundels have been set in a plain background for a repeating mosaic tile. W

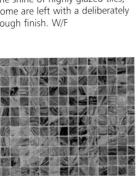

▲ **Oyster blue** The neutral shades here are reminiscent of the coastal elements – particularly driftwood and oyster shell. W

▲ **Contrasting grout** The pinkness of these peach tiles is emphasized by the lavender grout. W

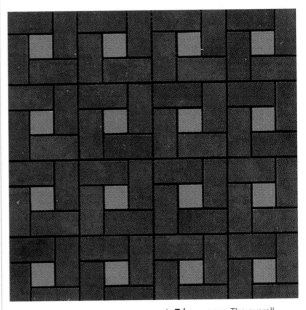

▲ **Trim weave** The overall tailored appearance of this smart basket-weave tile can be seen on page 166. W

▲ **Glass ovals** This is an unusual format for a glass mosaic tile, with ovals slotted together and fixed on a backing mesh. W

▲ **Blocks** The use of tones of the same stone colour give an extra dimension to this border. W/F

▲ **Brick bond** The staggered placing of the elements in this mosaic creates a brickwork effect. W

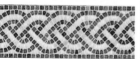

▲ **Mosaic borders** These borders are ready-made and would add the finishing touch to a floor made of plain terracotta or stone tiling. F

▲ **Classical style** Take inspiration from ancient civilizations and add unmistakable class with top-of-the-range polished marble. W/F

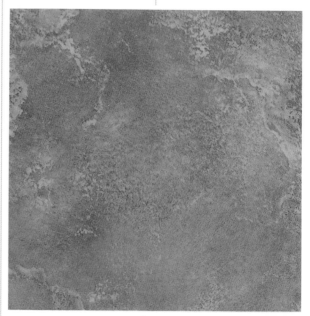

▲ **Traditional ceramic** This large-format ceramic makes for an elegant antique-style finish, and it can also be used as flooring surrounding a pool. F

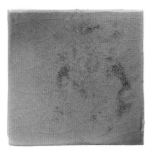

▲ **Milk chocolate** A hand-made tile in a handsome chocolate colour with a fine crackle finish to the glaze. W

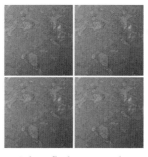

▲ **Colour flashes** Spots of colour can influence the appearance of the overall background colour, as the marble tile here shows. W/F

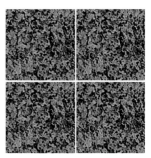

▲ **Spotted granite** A mixture of neutral shades and strong colour is attractive in a natural granite stone. F

▲ **Dark tan** The slightly lighter grout colour has been chosen carefully here, outlining the deep colour of the tiles. W

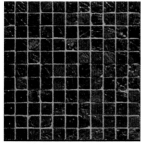

▲ **Bronzed green** If you want a neutral that packs a punch, try a blend of bronze-green with rusty brown. W

▲ **Neutral range** Neutral colours range from almost blacks to all kinds of off-whites, as this mosaic demonstrates. W

▲ **Porcelain border** An example of porcelain flooring tiles in both large and small formats. F

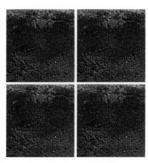

▲ **Neutral tones** Even the redness of natural terracotta can harbour yellow tones. F

▲ **Pebbles and fossils** Irregular border designs contrast with the regularity of square tiles. W

▲ **Dark geometric** A geometric floor design that avoids the use of terracottas and is instead based around light and dark neutrals. F

▲ **Pebble-effect floor** Pebbles attached to a backing can be used both inside and out. F

▲ **Crazy paving** Fifties style made easy, with a mosaic of crazy sizes that can be used like any other tile. W

▲ Simple border designs
Two classic borders based on simple square and rectangle shapes. W

▲ Inserted stripes
Border tiles and stripes can be repeated in various ways. W

▲ **Victorian** A roll-top bath with golden fittings has the perfect setting in this bathroom complete with tile trims, borders, panels and ceramic tile art. W/F

▲ **Linoleum tile** A swirling marble-effect linoleum can be a practical alternative to real stone flooring. F

▲ **Designer glass** The tile designers' art has been used to create a glass tile that resembles the inside of a seashell. W

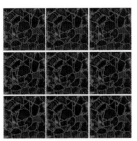

▲ **Dark glass** A recycled glass tile in a dark neutral green. This would combine well with other neutrals such as green-grey slate and stone. W

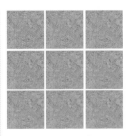

▲ **Cork tile** Cork tiling now comes in a wide range of colours, many based around the neutral palette. F

▲ **Natural flooring** The cream tiles shown here are ideal for emphasizing the richly coloured insets. F

▲ **Encaustic geometric border** This wide flooring border combines affordable geometric tiles with more expensive patterned encaustic tiles, which are used more sparingly, just as they were hundreds of years ago. F

▲ **Classic slate** This pale grey slate has a few lines of a warmer neutral within it. W/F

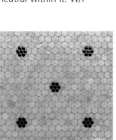

▲ **Cork mosaic** An unusual use of cork in a mosaic finish with black medallions on a neutral background. W/F

▲ **Compass point** Ideal for the centre of a large floor, this mosaic panel is ready to lay. F

▲ **Spanish stoneware** Unique combinations of colour result from a high-fire kiln technique, producing tiles suited to walls and floors. W/F

▲ **Building patterns** This arrangement is a stunning example of how a pattern can be built up using neutral natural stone. F

black and white

Black absorbs all light, and white reflects the maximum, so the combination of the two can be difficult to use without the end result being too stark or glaring. Luckily, true blacks and true whites are rare in tiles. Most have other subtle colours within them, giving a softer result and, when combined with greys and other neutrals, projecting an air of classic elegance.

black and white

Although black is said to be a funereal colour, black clothes are seen as elegant and glamorous, so a touch of black will always sharpen any colour scheme.

All-white can be clinical and stark, but the judicious use of white creates a sense of space and cleanness, so it's always a sound background colour for a kitchen or bathroom.

Greys (which are blacks and whites combined) are more user-friendly and versatile than black or white and deserve to be used more often. Greys used alongside black and white soften the relentless nature of the contrast.

Note that black, white and grey don't appear on the colour wheel as these are the true neutrals, with no colour in them. However, in real life, as mentioned, they often contain a little colour, appearing slightly pink or green, for example. Bear this in mind when you are matching colours and don't assume all blacks, whites and greys are the same. Grey stones, or imitation stones, can have a warm cast to them or a distinct cool, blue tone. Look for and use these qualities when putting together your scheme.

Greys tend to take on a little of the colours with which they are used. If you want to avoid an all-neutral scheme, mix them with sophisticated mauves and lilacs or with aquamarine or mint greens.

▶ Black and white can be fun as well as dramatic, and this chequered pattern is a design classic for any tiled area.

▲ The texture in this black tiling gives a wonderful sense of night-time glamour, with the tiny halogen spotlights in the ceiling enhancing the effect.

▲ **Charcoal** This charcoal Marmoleum would give a distinctive ambience. F

▲ **Black border** A suitable companion to a black and white bathroom scheme. W

▲ **City classic** Black and white geometric tiling makes up the path to the typical Victorian house, complete with the traditional stand-up rope edging tile. F

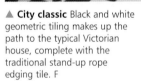

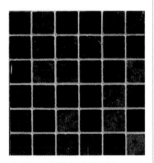

▲ **Textured black** Black in interiors often looks best when gently shaded and mottled rather than flat black. W

▲ **Pebble-effect tile** These pebbles have been carefully chosen for size and cleverly fixed to a backing so they can be laid just like a mosaic tile. F

▲ **Stone grey** Use colours from the warm spectrum in the rest of the room to set off this cool grey flooring tile. F

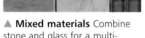

▲ **Mixed materials** Combine stone and glass for a multi-layered effect. W

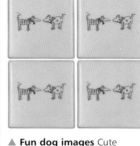

▲ **Fun dog images** Cute without being cutesy, these dog tiles would be perfect for the area around the dog's bed! W

▲ **Metro white** The bevelled edge of a metro-style tile gives a characteristic air of urban chic. W

▲ **Diamond border** A calm and simple design to put with matching stone tiles in a larger format. F

▲ **Textured white** Add some texture to an all-white scheme with this border. W

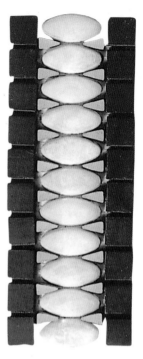

▲ **Opal white** The oval glass inserts in this border look like semi-precious stones but are tough enough to walk on. W/F

▲ **Shades of white** In the realm of home decorating, colours overlap in the spectrum, so be prepared to be spoilt for choice if you've decided on a "white" colour scheme – it might not be that simple! W

▲ **Resilient lino** Already hard-wearing, linoleum tiles in darker shades will be almost unspoilable. F

▲ **Gentler style** If you would prefer to avoid the severity of black and white, try dark grey-green with off-white for a softer look. F

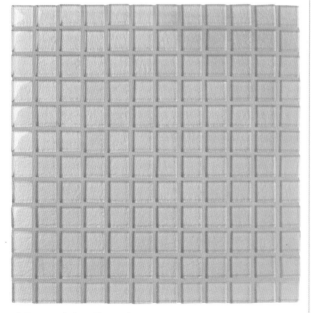

▲ **Pure and clear** The total simplicity and clarity of these glass tiles means that they have to be laid with great care to avoid leaving any unwanted air bubbles behind. W

▲ **Border twist** This could be added to a neutral stone floor or used to set off pale terracotta flooring. W/F

▲ **Dandelion** A soft floral design in the style of an etching or historical botanical print. W

▲ **Petal design** This makes a change from the usual repeating pattern of squares or rectangles and builds up to a fascinating surface. W

▲ **Leaf and tendril** This design has been used since medieval times as the basis for long decorative borders. F

▲ **Bathroom style** Large-format porcelain tiling covers the walls and floor of this bathroom, with mosaic breaking up the severe lines and glass and chrome as the contrast. W/F

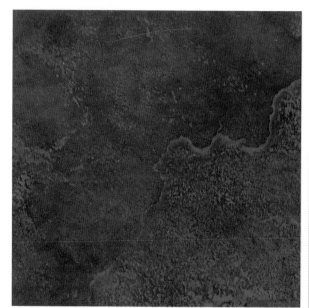

▲ **Tumbled edges** Many stone tiles are deliberately tumbled to give a relaxed, antique finish to them. W/F

▲ **Pure slate** It's hard to beat a pure grey slate for country houses, and it works in city homes too. F

▲ **Braid** An interwoven braid border is an option for an otherwise plain area of stone flooring. F

▲ **Dragonflies** Pictorial panels of 12 tiles are a style classic of the 19th century and are enjoying a revival. W

▲ **Ice cool** A perfect hand-crafted tile to give the impression of freshness and tranquility. W

▲ **Black and blue** Pure black glass is hard to find, but dark blue mosaic often has black elements to it. W

▲ **Black insert** The simplest of ideas are often the most effective – a small black insert breaks up an expanse of white. W/F

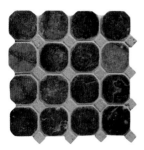

▲ **Almost black** The stones in this mosaic go from grey to almost black, and the putty-coloured insert gives a mellow look. W/F

▲ **Leaping dolphin** The ancient Greeks and Romans were fond of fish mosaics, especially of dolphins. This one comes ready-made. F

▲ **Faux stone** Imitations can be totally convincing and have the added bonus of being easier to maintain. F

▲ **Pure black** Absolute black is rare in nature, but this porcelain tile will supply it. W

▲ **Etched rose** Flower tiles are often coloured, so this is a chance to stay in simple black and white. W

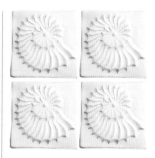

▲ **Spiral shell** Use plain white motif tiles sparingly as interesting accents, just as you would coloured ones. W

▲ **Kitchen chic** Subway or metro tiles are particularly suited to a city flat. W

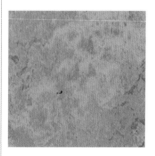

▲ **Dove grey** Different hues show how the home decorator's colour palette is open to interpretation. F

▲ **Linoleum tile** For a floor tile to make an understated background, this subtle pattern is the answer. F

▲ **Onions** A deep layer of white glaze brings out this onion design. W

▲ **Clay star** Black, blue-grey and off-white are joined with grout in a lighter grey. F

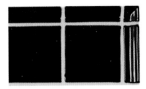

▲ **Ceramic black** The deepest of blacks in a ceramic tile with border tiles and corner trims to match. W

▲ **Scrolling black** A border that could be used with the black tiles above or with a mixture of black and white tiling. W

▲ **Glass trims** A line of trim tiles that would be particularly effective in an otherwise white bathroom. W

▲ **Border whites** Bright white border tiles add interest when the remainder of the tiling is plain. W

▲ **Subtle décor** The use of a field tile, rose motif and antique white border makes a subtle wall decoration. W

▲ **Printed tiles** Only when you have a significant area of these tiles can you appreciate the wallpaper effect of the cleverly repeating pattern. W

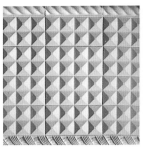

▲ **Timeless elegance** The geometric effect of these wall tiles is reminiscent of Victorian and Edwardian hall dado design. W

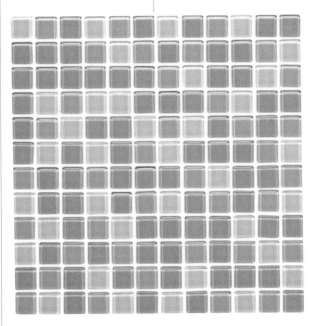

▲ **Cool and warm** A mixture of cool and warm greys has been amalgamated to make a glass mosaic that is adaptable for colour scheming. W

▲ **Small rectangular mosaic**
A repeating pattern leads the eye round the room. W

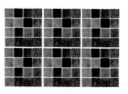

▲ **Graded greys** These mosaic squares give a softer effect than a block of tiles all in the same solid colour, which can be a relief when deocrating with a darker colour scheme. W

▲ **Bold stripes** Stripes with this degree of definition should be used with caution, but they make perfect splashbacks or panels. W

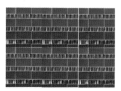

▲ **Mixed sizes** Tiles in slightly contrasting sizes build up to an attractive band effect along a wall. W

▲ **Tumbled marble** The finishing technique of tumbling rounds off the edges and corners. F

▲ **Classic white relief tiles**
A band of tiles in a simple relief pattern give a look of under-stated class to an area of plain white tiles. W

▲ **Shimmer** The subtle surface of these tiles adds interest to their simplicity. W

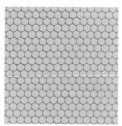

▲ **Unglazed mosaic** There is an unusual honeycomb shape to this mesh-backed mosaic tiling. The unglazed off-white finish has a matt texture that would appeal if you want a modern alternative to the more usual sheen of glazed tiles. W

▲ **Brushed basalt** This dark, fine-grained volcanic rock is extremely hard, so is suitable for internal and external application. W/F

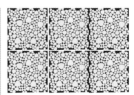

▲ **Porcelain pebbles** These modern mosaic tiles will give a clean and contemporary appearance to a kitchen or bathroom. W/F

▲ **Textural interest** Heavy relief decoration on glazed tiles in white and soft neutrals adds dimension to an area. W

▲ **Rich black stone** These rich dark stone tiles give a look of pure luxury yet are extremely hard wearing. W/F

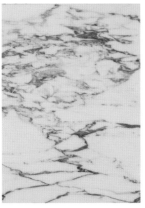

▲ **Blue veined** This is one of the most classic types of marble available. F

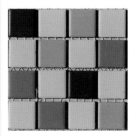

▲ **Brick bond** These mesh-backed tiles form a perfect brickwork effect, which is a modern twist on the traditional tile pattern. W

▲ **Pale slate** Dove-grey slate makes a perfect neutral background, and this one has a touch of pink warmth in the colouring. W/F

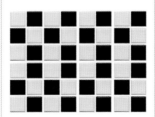

▲ **Chequered** You can't go wrong with this traditional combination as a border in a bathroom. W

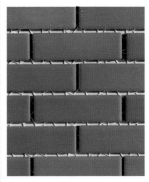

▲ **Porcelain mosaic** Tough tiles to give a neutral background to any hardworking area. W

▲ **Natural quarried slate** Vary the way tiles are cut and laid to achieve different looks, and use different grouts to highlight certain tones. F

▲ **Spanish copper glaze** These superior tiles give a truly regal look and are suited to the more opulent home. W

▲ **Black marble** This durable stone won't show any scratches, even in this dark shade. W/F

▲ **Polished granite** The toughest of all stone, granite is usually polished to a hard-wearing high-gloss finish. F

▲ **Patterned granite** This is a heavily patterned granite that would make a bold statement. F

▲ **Chequerboard** Careful attention has been paid to create a modern-looking border to this traditional black and white flooring design. F

metallics

Metallics produce an urban style of interior, whether in the form of rich iridescent mosaics or sleek pewter tiling. Metallics usually have a high light-reflecting quality, gleaming almost in the dark, with their ability to pick up and reflect any light that's going.

metallics

The metallic effect in tiles can be applied to almost any colour, making the surface stand out and the overall effect of the tiles much stronger and more noticeable. For this reason, this type of tile should be used with discretion, as too much could be distracting.

Underlying the sheen on the surface, metallic tiles divide into cool colours – silver, platinum, chrome and pewter – and warm colours – such as bronze and gold. They combine extremely well with almost all other types of tile and particularly with natural wood colours.

▲ This industrial-chic techno design has been adapted from flooring to make a repeating wall tile pattern. It would cover a large area impressively and would suit a contemporary kitchen in stainless steel or very pale wood.

▲ Metallic finishes don't have to be severe – here small squares in a soft metal finish have been combined with light-hearted accessories and wallpaper. The clear reflection in the surface creates the illusion of greater space in the room.

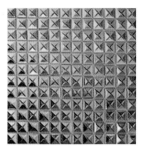  

▲ **True metallic** These two tiles are true metals embossed with a repeating stud design. They could be used in alternating panels with conventional tiling or mosaics. W

▲ **Pewter** The perfect imitation of a liquid metal portrayed on clever ceramic glaze. W

▲ **Metal flower** Metallic finishes can be discreet, as with this floral design. W

▲ **Copper finish** A bronzed, weathered copper effect in a ceramic tile. W

▲ **Aged metal** This tile has a scratch-effect surface that dulls the shine but not the overall aesthetic. W

▲ **Gold and silver** It is possible to successfully mix these two colours, as this glass mosaic shows, with other metallics dispersed between them. W

▲ **Stove metals** Metallic tiles fit effortlessly into kitchens, particularly stove splashbacks, echoing the metals used in the utensils and the stove itself. W

▲ **Lustre** Tile-makers have learned how to imitate the rich lustre of metal in glaze, with magical results. W

▲ **Golden glints** This glass mosaic has a very silvery hue, with gold flashes as it catches the light. W

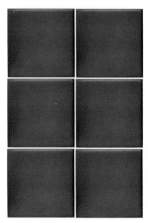

Metal inserts These three metal tiles, above and below, are designed to be used as inserts for tile flooring patterns. Perhaps surprisingly, they work exceptionally well with terracotta tiles, where they make a lovely contrast with the surrounding reds and oranges. F

▲ **Metal with blue** Metals often give off colours as the light catches them, such as this brilliant blue. W

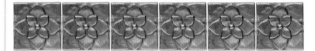

▲ **Midas touch** A glittering golden stud tile for a touch of pure Hollywood glamour. W

▲ **Smooth porcelain** The aged effect on this tile would make it suitable for a study or library. W/F

▲ **Glazed graphite** The copper-based glaze in this type of tile is only suited to dry areas, as it can otherwise be prone to discolouration. W

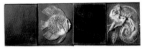

▲ **Handmade glazed** The unusual fish and chameleon images on these tiles would be best suited to a house in warm climates. W

▲ **Coal black** Take care with the lighting in the room to make the most of the reflective qualities of this mosaic. W

▲ **Glass lozenge** A glass strip with a metallic sheen to insert among plain tiling. W

▲ **Picture frame** This tile has a metallic glazed frame around the central design. W

▲ **Priceless** The bright surface of this tile gives the illusion of a precious metal. W

▲ **Copper** A warm copper with an antique effect spreading over the surface. W

▲ **Etched leaf** There are hidden colours of turquoise and lilac in this metallic surface, which could be used to complete the room scheme. W

▲ **Insert squares** Tough metal inserts designed for flooring patterns. F

▲ **Darkest metal** This dark and rich surface needs spotlighting, but avoid overlighting it. W

▲ **Auburn lights** A copper metallic finish that is almost red. Try combining this with blacks or creams. W

▲ **Tiling inserts** These little tiles are not intended to be used over a large area but intermittently as inserts in areas of stone or terracotta, where their metallic shine will form a fine contrast to their rough matt finish. F

▲ **Sheen** A metallic finish with a delicate sheen to it, rather than a gleaming shine, gives a more elegant look. W

▲ **Metal and glass** Metals and glass have a natural affinity, as these glass inserts in a wall of metallic tiling demonstrates. W

▲ **Pale gold** This palest of golden glazes could be combined with other metallic-finish tiles. W

▲ **Mottled silver** The patchiness of solid colour here will create a softer ambience in a room. W

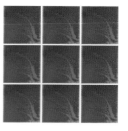

▲ **Gold stud** An unusual bright gold and black tile, which would make a dramatic border to a simpler black field tile. W

▲ **Mother-of-pearl** Metallic finishes can be soft and warm, as demonstrated by the beautiful pink and white effect of this rectangular tile. W

▲ **Metallic leaf** A subtle use of the metallic effect here, based around a soft leaf design and pretty colours. W

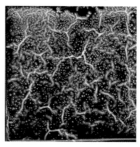

▲ **Charcoal grey** This charcoal hue would work well blended with stone and slate, with the slight flame effect in the design. W

▲ **Crackle finish** This crackle-glaze effect is striking on a black metallic tile and would look good as a splashback, or combined with black granite countertops. W

▲ **Gloss glazed** Combine with coordinating plain, similarly glazed field tiles to form a pattern border or as drop-ins. W

▲ **Spanish copper glaze** These superior tiles give a truly regal look and are suited to the more opulent home. W

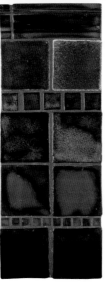

▲ **Copper ceramic** A copper finish would look good in a kitchen where copper decorative items are on display. W

▲ **Gold medallion** This design is associated with classical European architecture and would be particularly effective as a fire surround, reflecting the light and flames. W

▲ **Exotic bronze** The bright bronze of these tiles would create an exotic effect in a bathroom or bedroom. W

▲ **Sculpted shell** Field tiles in jewel-rich colorus combined with shell-shaped mouldings form a bold horizontal effect. W

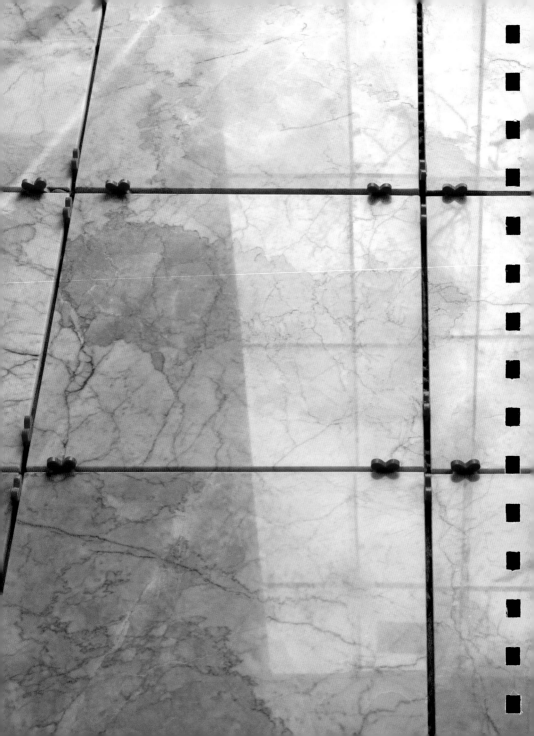

the techniques

Once you've chosen the colour and material of your tiles, you'll need to give some thought to their installation. Like most DIY projects, successful tiling is dependent on careful planning, having the right tools for the job and following some basic practical steps.

Tiling walls and work surfaces is not particularly difficult, as long as you are prepared to take time to get it right. A splashback or countertop is a good project for a beginner to learn the techniques before tackling something more complex, like a window surround.

Tiling floors, however, is hard work, and you might want to contact a specialist flooring contractor. Many suppliers can recommend suitable contractors who offer a complete service – from attending to the subfloor to final sealing.

Materials
Stones, slates and porcelain tiles can be difficult to cut without professional cutting tools, and they are difficult to manœuvre. Extreme care is needed when cutting glass tiles.

Resilient flooring, such as linoleum, vinyl and cork, are within the grasp of a good amateur home renovator, though planning and organization are still needed to avoid expensive mistakes.

Cost
If money is an issue, the cost of materials needs to be balanced by the difficulty of installation. The price of money saved by not hiring professionals may be a ruined floor. Don't forget to budget for buying or hiring tools and purchasing material for the subfloor.

There are two main areas for tiling in the home, and this practical how-to section addresses them both in full:
Walls, pages 213–231
Floors, pages 232–249

adhesives and grout

All tiles need fixing in place with some form of adhesive or mortar. Resilient tiles are usually close-fitted with no spaces between them, and you simply use the adhesive that's recommended by the tile manufacturer. Most of the advice in this section refers to hard tiles that are laid with gaps between them and then grouted. Grout finishes off most hard-tiled surfaces: it prevents water and dirt from penetrating the gaps between the tiles. Tiles are grouted after they have been in place for 12–24 hours (refer to the tile adhesive package for the exact timing). Grout is usually a neutral colour, but coloured grout is available, which defines the tiles as part of the design.

The choice of grout colour and the width of the joint will have a big impact on the final appearance of your tiled surface.

Spacing

Grout is used partly to hold tiles firmly in place and partly because the edges of tiles are rarely a perfect fit without gaps. Grouting spaces vary according to the look required.

The minimum joint is about 3 mm (⅛ inch) and gives a precise, contemporary look to modern tiles, like porcelain.

Some floor tiles (like terracotta) can have grouting as wide as 2 cm (¾ inch). However, very wide grouting can crack.

Spacers regulate the gaps and keep the tiles from moving while the adhesive or mortar dries. You can use matchsticks or pieces of cardboard, but the easiest option is to buy packs of inexpensive plastic spacers that are available in various sizes to create different widths of grout lines. Traditional spacers are pegs that are removed once the adhesive or mortar has set, but you can also get spacers that can be left in place and simply grouted over.

Dos and don'ts

> Some grout and adhesive comes ready mixed in a tub. The majority come in powder form and get mixed with water to make a paste.

> Powdered grout is either sanded or non-sanded. Sanded grouts are for wider grout joints (i.e. floors) of 3 mm (⅛ inch) upward. Non-sanded grout is usually only for wall-tile installations.

> Don't mix more than you can use before it sets (setting times range from 30 minutes to a few hours). Don't add more water if it starts to set – throw it out and start again.

> An epoxy grout should be used for countertops because it's impervious to spills and acids.

> Waterproof grout must be used in a shower area and around a bath or sink, otherwise mould will form.

> Don't let the grout harden on the front of the tiles. Wipe the tiles frequently and rinse the cloth or sponge often to avoid smears.

> Where the tiles butt up to an adjoining surface (e.g. a bath, sink or countertop), do not grout the join but seal it with a silicone or acrylic sealant after the grout has dried fully. This will allow for a slight movement. If working on a bath, stand in the bath as you seal the join so that the joint will accommodate your body weight.

> When grouting a floor, start from the corner furthest from the door, cleaning off the tops of the tiles as you work your way across.

> Don't allow people to walk on a newly grouted floor. After grouting, apply one or more further coats of sealant/polish as appropriate.

> A grout sealant can also be applied to help stop it going dirty and grey over time.

Adhesive or mortar?

Adhesive is simpler to use than mortar. It's supplied ready-mixed and can be applied directly from the container.

Mortar must be mixed in a bucket, sets faster than adhesive and isn't recommended for wooden subfloors because it may rot the wood. Mortar is cheaper than adhesive however, and is usually used for large, heavy stone tiles.

Some manufacturers produce a fast-setting, multipurpose product that can be used both as an adhesive and a grout, enabling you to tile and grout in a single day. However, these products are not suitable for all applications.

Porcelain tiles are fired at very high temperatures. This makes them virtually non-porous. It's important to use an adhesive specifically designed for porcelain, which cures, rather than sets by drying out.

Technical advances mean there is now a wide range of grouts and adhesives on the market, from the traditional sand and cement to high-performance materials. The golden rule is to ask the tile supplier for their recommended type of grout and adhesive for the tiles in question.

Epoxy grout

If your tiles will come into contact with water (e.g. in bathrooms and showers), or if there are hygiene issues (e.g. on kitchen countertops), then an epoxy grout is recommended. More expensive than traditional grouts, these are two-part systems that form a very hygienic and impermeable finish once they have set. They should also be used for metal tiles. Care is needed to remove the grout residue as you go, however, because it's difficult to get rid of once it's set (though you can get a special grout remover). Wear suitable gloves – epoxy grout shouldn't come into direct contact with skin.

Tile spacers Spacers ensure even grout lines between tiles. Matchsticks or pieces of cardboard can be used, but plastic spacers are inexpensive, easy to use and available in a variety of sizes to suit your particular tile project.

tools

Most of the tools needed for tiling and surface preparation are general-purpose household tools you may already have. If not, they are readily available at a hardware shop.

However, it's worth getting a few specialist pieces of equipment to make your tiling project go smoothly. Hardware shops now stock lots of tools that make cutting and shaping tiles easier. The only problem that may arise is with very hard or thick tiles, such as ceramics or stones, and then you may have to hire or borrow professional cutting machinery.

Hammer

Scraper

Grout saw

Sandpaper

Pencil

Tape measure

Felt-tipped pen

Protective gloves

Steam stripper

Cordless drill

Grout float

Safety goggles

Short spirit level

Long spirit level

Cutting

Tile nippers

Tile saw

Workbench

Tile-cutting machine

Tile cutter

Tile pliers

Tiling

Grout spreader

Small-notched spreader

Sponge

Grout shaper

Cold chisel

Cotton rag

Sealant gun

Tile file

Trowel

Large-notched spreader

Tile spacers

Safety equipment

> When budgeting for the project, don't skimp on safety equipment. Handling the tools and equipment can be dangerous.

> Strong rubber gloves will protect your hands from materials like levelling compound, adhesive, sealant and varnish.

> Strong work gloves will protect your hands when handling rough, heavy tiles and tiles with cut edges.

> Safety glasses protect the eyes from flying shards when using electric tools or preparing surfaces.

> Ear protectors should be worn when using electric tools.

> Facemasks prevent the inhalation of dust, and some protect against potentially harmful fumes. Always work in a well-ventilated area.

ordering

Following a few golden rules when it comes to ordering your tiles can help to avoid disappointment regarding stock and ensure that you don't fall short for your tiling project.

Tiles vary from batch to batch during production. The display sample you have been given by your supplier may be quite old. It's worth asking to see a brand new sample before you decide.

Play it safe

If you can afford it, it's sensible to order an extra box of tiles – or at least five or six extra – to put away for the future. Tiles are becoming high-fashion items with quickly changing styles. It is highly likely that the tiles you have chosen today will simply not be available in five years' time. If a tile gets damaged or if you later remodel your kitchen or bathroom, you'll have peace of mind knowing that you have a few extra tiles safely stored away for just this occasion.

Tiles are quite fragile items. They often reach you after a long journey. Check them thoroughly as soon as they arrive because many shippers will only give you a limited time to claim for damage and breakages. Make sure the tiles are the correct size, the correct shade and come from the same dye lot or batch number, so that you are satisfied they will blend together.

The exact colour of tiles can't be guaranteed from one batch to the next. Make sure you order enough tiles the first time around. It's a good idea to allow for 10 per cent extra tiles in case of breakages, mistakes and wastage due to cutting.

Variations

Tile samples from the showroom may have been sealed and finished to show you what the final surface will look like. Of course, your own tiles will not resemble these until you seal and finish them accordingly.

Spend time loose laying the tiles to get the most attractive colour distribution before fixing them down. You, or your tiler, should also shuffle the contents of the tile boxes to even out any colour variations.

Thresholds

Remember to plan the transition from a tiled floor to the flooring in the next room. The levels may differ dramatically, and a threshold-reducer strip may be needed (this usually happens in a doorway). Thresholds are available in lots of different materials, but some look better than others. A classic wooden bar would look better against an expensive tiled floor than something made of shiny metal or plastic.

Trimming doors

Doors may need trimming to fit the new floor height. Check that your contractor will include this in the job (not all of them do).

ESTIMATING THE NUMBER OF TILES

tile size (centimetres)	approx. number of tiles per square metre	tile size (inches)	approx. number of tiles per square yard
10 x 10	100	4 x 4	81
15 x 15	45	6 x 6	36
20 x 15	34	8 x 6	27
20 x 20	25	8 x 8	21
20 x 25	20	8 x 10	17
20 x 30	17	8 x 12	14
30 x 30	12	12 x 12	9

walls

Creating a sound, level surface on which to tile is essential. Not only will this produce better results when new tiles are applied, it will also make the tiling process much easier. A new wall surface is the ideal starting point for tiling, but it is often the case that an old tiled surface is being replaced.

Existing tiles

A previously tiled surface can be tiled over if it is sound and level. If the old tiles are firmly stuck to the wall, new tiles may be applied directly over the top of them. Some minor repairs may be necessary to ensure that the surface is totally sound. Remove any loose old tiles before beginning the preparation.

I Fill the space left by the removal of old tiles with an all-purpose crack filler. Before applying the filler, dust out the hole thoroughly to ensure good adhesion. Build up the filler until it is level and flush with the surrounding tiles.

2 An alternative to using filler in the space left by loose old tiles is to use old tiles of the same size as those on the wall. Simply apply some adhesive to the tile and use it to fill the hole. Again, make sure that the tile surface is flush with the surrounding area of tiles.

3 After the old tiled surface has been filled, wash it down with soapy water, then rinse well. Sand the entire tiled area with silicone carbide paper; this will scratch the glaze and help provide a key for the adhesive. Make sure that you sand each tile to get the best possible adhesion of new tile to old.

Safety first

> Wear appropriate safety equipment, like hand and eye protection and a facemask against dust, when preparing surfaces. If in doubt, call in the professionals.

boxing in

As well as wall surfaces, there are other areas that may require preparation before you can start tiling. Unsightly pipes, for example, can be boxed in and then the box can be tiled to create a decorative surface.

Simple boxing

Boxing in requires a combination of wooden supports and building board to build a sturdy framework around the pipes. Water-resistant medium-density fibreboard 18 mm ($^3/_4$ inch) thick is ideal, with 5 x 2.5 cm (2 x 1 inch) wood strips as support. Boxing is best screwed together rather than nailed to provide stronger joints.

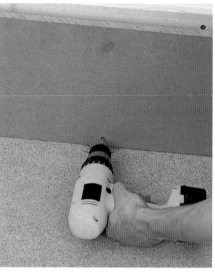

2 Cut a sheet of board to the correct size. The height should be the same as that of the top edge of the wall support. Screw the sheet in place at floor level, allowing the screw to go through the board and into the floor support.

1 Attach a support to the wall directly above the pipes and secure another support to the floor. Make sure the floor support runs parallel to the wall surface, and that it is positioned further away from the wall than the pipe. Use screws that do not go below the level of the floorboards, otherwise you may damage pipes or cables below floor level or, even more importantly, you may injure yourself.

COVERED UP
Although accuracy is important, remember that the boxing will be covered, so a perfect finish at this stage is not essential.

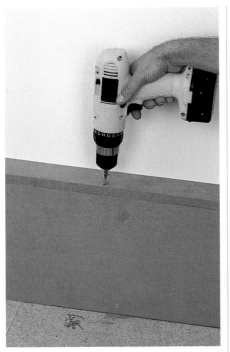

CUTTING CURVES

Use a jigsaw to cut curves in the board where you need to allow pipes to protrude through the boxing. When using a jigsaw, always follow all the manufacturer's safety recommendations and never place your hand in front of the blade or in the direction in which you are cutting.

3 Cut a second piece of board and attach it to the wall support and first sheet of board. Make sure that the corner joint is precise in order to achieve a neat finish. Continue until the pipes are totally boxed in and the box is ready to tile.

CORNER BOXING

Corners may be either boxed in (as shown above, but vertically), or a single panel can be used to cover the corner, as shown left. This method requires making a mitred cut through a length of wood at a 45-degree angle and creating an angled support to which a corner junction can be attached. A thin building board, such as water-resistant plywood, can then be cut to fit across the corner. Attach the plywood to the supports using brads or small screws.

LEAVING ACCESS

Many pipes have shut-off valves, stopcocks or inspection joints, depending on the particular function of the pipe. You need to make inspection hatches in the boxing to allow access to these points. Cutting in a small hatch and fitting it with a magnetic catch is the ideal solution.

starting level

Tiles have crisp straight edges that give a very ordered and precise finish when they are applied to the wall. Although this is one of their attractive characteristics, it also means that poorly applied or crooked tiles stand out, so it is important to start level and tile from a secure, fixed base. Take time to determine the starting point, as mistakes can be difficult to rectify once tiling has begun.

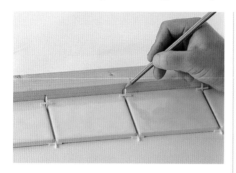

1 A tiling gauge is essential for determining the best possible starting point on a wall surface. This is the starting point for the entire design. Cut a 5 x 2.5 cm (2 x 1 inch) piece of wood about 1.5 m (5 feet) long, or shorter if you are tiling a small area. Line up a row of tiles along the length of this wood with tile spacers between them. Using a pencil, mark the position of each tile along one edge of the wood.

2 Find the central point of the wall or area to be tiled by measuring first vertically and then horizontally. Make sure that the tape measure is level when measuring. Make a pencil mark at the centre.

3 Use the tiling gauge to figure out how many rows of tiles you will need for the area you are going to tile. Hold the gauge vertically against the wall to show where the tile edges will fall once they are applied. Mark the positions along the wall. Then hold the gauge horizontally and mark again. It is unlikely that the tiles will fit exactly into the working area, so you will need to adjust the central starting point slightly so that any tiles you have to cut will be at the edges and not in the centre.

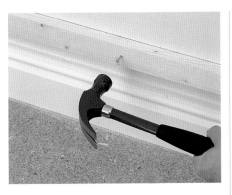

4 It is unlikely that the top of the baseboard is exactly level, or that the tile gauge has demonstrated that the best position to start tiling is directly on top of it. The bottom row of tiles will probably require cuts. This means that the starting point is where the first row of full tiles will be applied, and this is where a length of wood should be secured to provide a solid base. Ensure that this support is level.

5 Once the horizontal support is secured, attach a vertical support to provide the starting point across the other wall dimension. Secure it where the first column of vertical tiles will begin, using a level to make sure that it is completely vertical. Alternatively, the vertical support can be positioned at the central point of the area to be tiled, and tiling can progress towards the corner, rather than away from it. Either way is acceptable, as the sole purpose of the vertical support is to maintain a rigid vertical line to butt the tiles up against.

6 Attach the wall supports with nails, but do not drive them all the way into the wall. Leave a good length of the nail head showing, so that the nails can be removed with a claw hammer and the support taken off once the tiles have been applied and the adhesive has set. Long masonry nails usually work well as they are sturdy enough to be driven into most wall types, and have a large head for easy removal. On dry walls or stud walls though, nails may not fix the batten firmly enough, in which case it is better to use screws.

applying adhesive

Tile adhesive must be applied evenly to ensure that
the tiles sit correctly on the wall surface. You can
use ready-mixed adhesive or powder that needs
water added to it. Both types are equally effective,
and there is no difference in technique when
applying them.

Small areas

In small, intricate tiling areas, it is easier if you
use smaller tools. You can apply the adhesive to
the wall or to the back of the tiles. Adhesive
starts to harden once it is exposed to the air, so
applying it to a small area at a time reduces the
possibility of it drying before the tile has been
applied to the wall.

APPLYING ADHESIVE TO TILES

Use a small notched spreader to apply adhesive
directly to the back of the tiles, removing any
excess. The jagged teeth of the spreader create an
even layer of peaks and troughs along the adhesive
surface, which improves adhesion when the tile is
applied to the wall.

GETTING INTO CORNERS

A small notched spreader is the ideal tool for
getting adhesive into tight corners. This is
especially useful when laying the first tiles,
which will need to be tight against the
supporting frame. Beginners will also find that
a small notched spreader is easier to use and
creates less mess than a large one.

Large areas

On large, open expanses of wall, tile adhesive can
be spread over greater areas of the wall surface,
and the tiles can be applied relatively quickly. Use a
large notched trowel since it covers a large wall
space much more quickly than a small spreader.

| Use the flat, broad surface of the notched
trowel to dig adhesive out of its tub or bucket,
then use a pressing, sweeping motion to apply it
to the wall. Do not try to apply too much at a
time, as the adhesive will simply fall away around
the sides of the trowel and onto the floor.

ADHESIVE ADVICE

When taking a break, always keep the lid on
the tub of tile adhesive to prevent it from
drying out.

If tiling a large area, use tile adhesive that
requires mixing, as it is usually cheaper than
ready-mixed varieties.

For very small areas, use tile and grout adhesive
since, as the name suggests, it can be used as
grout as well as adhesive. Although it tends to
be expensive, it is very economical in small
areas as it eliminates the need to buy both an
adhesive and a grout, which are difficult to
buy separately in the small quantities you
would need.

2 Draw the serrated edge of the trowel across
the surface of the adhesive, creating furrows
in its surface. Apply enough pressure for the points
along the trowel's edge to touch the wall surface,
but not enough for them to gouge into it. This
creates an even coat that is the ideal surface to
twist the first tiles onto, producing a firm bond
between wall and tiles.

3 Do not cover more than one square metre (or
one square yard) of the wall at a time, because
the tiles must be applied while the adhesive is still
wet and workable. It is better for beginners to start
by covering an area half this size and gradually
build up to the larger area.

applying the first tiles

The first tiles are the most important in any tile design because they provide the starting point and base for the whole tiled area. Poor application at this stage can affect the entire finish, so you need to take great care when positioning the first tiles.

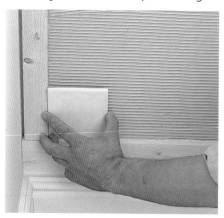

1 Place the first tile tight into the corner made by the horizontal and vertical support frame edges. Use a slight twisting motion when pressing the tile onto the adhesive surface to ensure good suction between the back of the tile and the adhesive.

2 Continue to apply tiles in a row along the top of the horizontal frame edge. Apply spacers between every tile to ensure uniform gaps for grouting. Because of the wooden frame, the spacers at the base of the first row of tiles have to be positioned pointing out from the tiled surface. These can be removed when the adhesive has set, whereas other spacers on the wall surface are left in position to be grouted over.

3 After every two rows of tiles, check that the level is being maintained. Use a short spirit level, held across three tiles at a time, to make sure that no tiles have slipped out of position. Take care not to get any tile adhesive on the level – clean it immediately if you do.

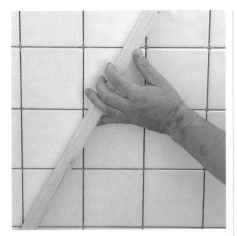

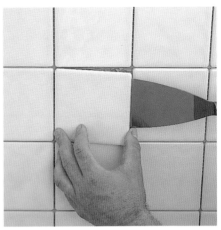

4 Once a larger block of tiles is complete, hold a long strip of wood across the tiled surface to check that they are all sitting flush. Any sunken or protruding tiles will be obvious and then any necessary adjustments can be made.

5 Adjustments to tile position must be carried out while the adhesive is still wet. Lever out sunken or protruding tiles with a scraper, being careful not to scratch or chip the tile surface.

Adhesive tips

> Use a damp rag or sponge to clean excess tile adhesive off the tiled surface as you go.

> Tile up to 1 m (1 yard) high, then allow the adhesive to set before applying any more tiles.

> Once the whole area has been tiled, the wooden frame must be left in place until the adhesive has set. Then remove it and use cut tiles to fill the gaps.

6 For a sunken tile, apply more adhesive to the back of the tile with a small notched spreader. Reposition the tile on the wall, again using the strip of wood to check that it is now sitting flush with the surrounding tiled surface. For a protruding tile, simply remove some of the adhesive and reapply the tile to the wall.

cutting tiles

To complete almost any tiling project, you will need to cut some tiles to fill gaps. Cutting a straight line across a tile is easy, and you can use one of two tools – a simple handheld tile cutter or a tile-cutting machine. Both will produce the same result.

Most wall tiles have a glazed surface and are fairly brittle. If the glazed surface has been scored, the tile should snap along the scored line.

Cutting and drilling porcelain tiles is much more difficult than standard ceramic tiles. Professional cutting and drilling machinery is needed. You can often hire these.

Floor tiles

You will need to buy or rent a special floor-tile cutter. For heavy tiles, an angle grinder is the best tool to use. You'll need a proper work surface or workbench. These tools need careful handling. Always wear protective clothing, including boots, and support the tile on a sturdy surface. (See pages 238–241 for more details on cutting floor tiles.)

Glass

Always use hand and eye protection when working with glass tiles. To cut glass tiles cleanly, you may need a wet saw with a diamond blade. Wet saws can be rented, but the blades will have to be bought. Because glass tiles are transparent, any crack in the tile is clearly visible. Most manufacturers advise using a crack-suppression membrane under the tiles. There needs to be an even coat of adhesive on the back of the tile to avoid rib lines showing through – "back

buttering" is recommended. Check for air pockets that could cause the tile to crack.

Metal

Metal tiles can be cut with saw blades especially designed to cut metal. Most manufacturers advise strongly against using power or rotating saw blades but recommend handsaws. Be cautious of resulting sharp edges – these can be deburred with a file. Some metal tiles are composites of metal with resin or ceramic bases – consult the manufacturers for their recommendations on cutting if

you are in doubt. Do not remove any protective covering from the tiles until the installation (including grouting) is complete.

Simple cutting

Using a handheld tile cutter is the more traditional method of cutting tiles. Their simple design combines a handle with a cutting spike that scores the tile as it is drawn across the tile surface. It is worth spending a little extra to get a good-quality tile cutter as these produce the cleanest cuts.

Cutting tips

> Don't mark the back of a tile with pen. In time, the ink can seep through to the front of the tile.

> Tile-cutting machines are available at DIY shops. These are inexpensive and make scoring and cutting much more reliable.

> If you need to drill a hole in a ceramic tile, do it after the tile is in position. Use a special tile bit, a low drill speed, and protect your eyes and hands from the powdered glaze that will fly off.

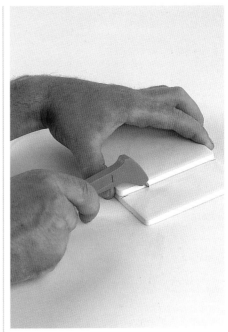

I Measure the distance between the edge of the tile and the corner junction to determine the size of tile needed to fill the gap. Take 3 mm (⅛ inch) off the measurement to allow for grout.

2 Mark the measurement on a full tile with a felt-tipped pen. Using another tile as a straight edge, score along the marked line with the tile cutter, applying a firm but even pressure. This will cut into the glazed surface of the tile, leaving a clearly defined scratch.

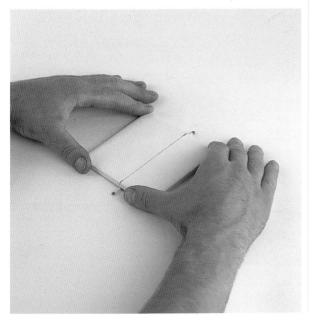

3 Place the scored tile on two matchsticks so that the "cut" line is positioned on the centre of each matchstick. Apply even downward pressure on each side of the scored line in order to snap the tile along the "cut" line.

Machine cutting

Tile cutting machines are a more recent innovation. Although they produce the same result as a handheld cutter, they tend to be quicker to use and, with practice, generally provide a more efficient way of cutting tiles. The same "scoring" principle is used, except the cutting blade is circular rather than a single cutting point.

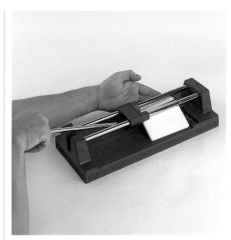

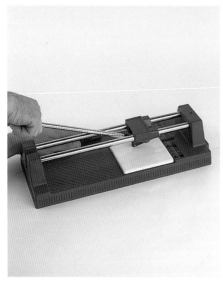

1 With a felt-tipped pen, mark where the cut is required and position the tile on the cutting machine so that the cutting wheel sits directly on the mark when lowered onto the tile. Applying an even downward pressure on the machine handle, push the cutting wheel along the full extent of the marked line, scratching the tile surface.

2 Clamp the tile between the bracket above the cutting wheel and below the two sliding rails. The scored line on the tile must be positioned centrally between the rails – most machines have a pointer on the cutting machine bracket so you can line it up accurately. Push down on the cutting-machine handle to snap the tile along the scored line.

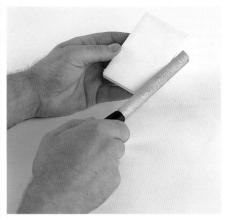

3 Most tile cuts will be clean and precise; if there are any rough edges or bumps, they can be removed with a tile file.

internal corners

Internal corners are the most common obstacle when tiling – quite simply because all rooms have them. If tiles are being laid on more than one wall in a room, you will have to deal with a corner. Tiling a corner is straightforward as long as you follow a few simple rules.

Simple cornering

If a tiling plan has been worked out correctly (see page 16), when you arrive at an internal corner you will usually require just under, or just over, half a tile to fill the gap between the last full tile and the corner junction. Cutting straight lines on the tiles is a simple process, and it is easy to produce a neatly tiled internal corner.

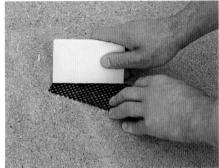

2 Tile the adjacent wall up to the corner junction. This wall will also need to be finished with a column of cut tiles. It is important to cut these as neatly as possible, as the cut edge of these tiles will overlap the column of tiles on the first wall. Remove any rough edges with a tile file or sanding strip, as above.

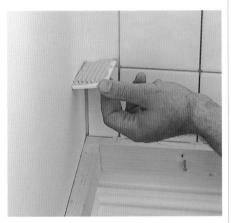

1 It is usually easier to apply the tile adhesive to the back of a cut tile, rather than the wall, when positioning the tiles along the corner junction. Make sure that the factory edge of the tile is jointed next to the column of full tiles, and the cut edge is running along the corner junction. Continue up the corner junction, filling the gap with more cut tiles.

3 Position the cut tiles along the corner junction and continue until the whole internal corner is tiled. Apply adhesive to cut tiles one at a time – don't apply it along the entire corner junction.

keeping tiles level

It is important to constantly check that tiles are level when dealing with an internal corner. Since cut tiles are just as likely to slip out of position as whole tiles, making sure that they stay in the correct place is essential for a neat finish. You need a spirit level and spacers to help you maintain the level across a corner.

1 Check that the tiles are in the correct position by holding a spirit level across the corner junction. Position the edge of the spirit level so that one end is at the junction between two tiles on one wall, while the other end is on the corresponding row of tiles on the adjacent wall.

2 Position spacers along the corner so that they span the junction and maintain the necessary gap between, and along, the two columns of cut tiles.

Cutting slivers

Sometimes small gaps along a corner will require thin slivers of tile to fill them. Because tiles are brittle, cutting a sliver using the usual cutting technique may break the tile. You need to use a slightly different technique, which puts a greater, more even pressure along the scored cutting line.

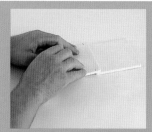

1 Measure the cut requirements as normal, then score the line with a handheld cutter or tile-cutting machine.

2 Rest the edge of the tile on top of another tile, making sure the scored line is positioned directly above the edge of the tile below. Apply even downward pressure on the main body of the scored tile until the sliver snaps off.

external corners

Internal corner joints overlap and are easy to conceal, while external joints are more prominent and expose any mistakes far more readily. Tiling an external corner is an exercise in concealment, which requires a slightly different tiling technique.

Plastic quadrants

The greatest aid to producing a neat external corner is plastic quadrant lipping. It creates a smooth defined edge to tile up to, and protects the corner from being knocked or chipped. Always try to plan your tiling strategy so that full tiles are used to tile away from the external corner.

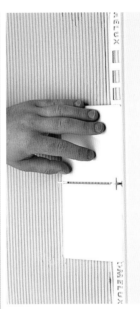

I Cut the quadrant to the required length with a hacksaw. Apply adhesive to one wall surface and align the quadrant precisely along the external corner edge. Make sure there is enough adhesive along the edge of the corner to hold the quadrant in position.

2 Tile the one wall, positioning the first tile next to the quadrant and butting it up tightly against the quadrant lip. Continue to apply tiles. Insert tile spacers along the quadrant–tile junction perpendicular to the tile surface, as the quadrant edge will not allow them to be laid flush against the wall surface. (These spacers can be removed when the adhesive is set.)

3 Once one wall is complete, apply adhesive to the adjacent wall and continue to tile that wall in the same way.

grouting and polishing

Once the tile adhesive has dried, you need to fill in the junctions between the tiles with grout to make the tiled surface water-resistant. As well as being practical, grout provides the overall finish, effectively framing the tiles and highlighting their decorative appeal.

Applying grout

Grout can be bought either ready-to-use or in a powder form that requires mixing with water. Both will produce the same result, although it is usually more economical to buy the powder form.

1 Mix grout in a clean bucket with cold water. Proportions will vary between manufacturers, but try to achieve a smooth, workable paste. If you mix by hand, it is easier to break up any lumps in the mixture. Always wear protective gloves since prolonged exposure to grout can cause skin irritation.

2 Apply the grout to the tiled surface using a grout spreader or squeegee. Use broad, sweeping movements in all directions to ensure that the grout gets into every joint. Grout small areas at a time since there is a fairly short working time before the grout starts to go hard, and it can be tricky to remove grout from the surface of the tiles once it has dried.

3 Remove the excess grout from the tiles with a damp sponge. Build up a rhythm of wiping off tiles and rinsing the sponge in clean water. Continue until all the grout is removed from the surface of the tiles, leaving just the grout in the junctions between the tiles.

4 Run the rounded end of a grout shaper along all the tile junctions to give the grout a final smooth surface, making each grouted joint into a perfect, slightly concave trough.

finishing off

Once the grout has dried, you need to check to make sure that the surface is watertight and that there are no grout splashes. It is almost inevitable that the odd area will need some minor attention, or that some grout will have found its way onto the tiled surface.

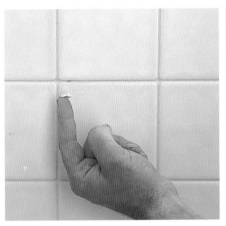

1 As the grout dries, air bubbles inside it can come to the surface and create a hole. If this happens, use the end of your finger to apply a small amount of grout to the hole to make the junction waterproof again.

2 Dried grout on the tiled surface can be removed using a scraper, but take care not to scratch the ceramic surface of the tile with the sharp edge of the scraper. Allow the scraper to slide along the surface of the tile, rather than digging down into the ceramic.

3 Finally, polish the tiles with a dry cotton rag to remove any powdery residue created by the wet grout being applied. You may need to do this two or three times on each area of tiles to remove all the residue and leave a clean, bright surface.

sealing wall tiles

Glazed tiles, of course, don't need sealing, though the grout might, unless you've chosen one that's waterproof. Sealing grout prevents water penetration and helps prevent staining, which can be particularly important with mosaic tiles or kitchen countertops with many grout lines.

However, in general, tiles and grouts with a porous surface need to be sealed after laying. An appropriate sealer should be purchased when you order your tiles.

Some sealants form a surface layer that then needs a further sacrificial layer of acrylic tile finish. This protects the sealant from being scraped off. The wear layer needs to be maintained, though, otherwise the sealant itself will be damaged and have to be removed and replaced.

Products are also available that are designed to enhance the surface colour of your tiles (in many cases, though, the sealer itself will do that).

Don't mix and match different products. Every surface is slightly different, and it's important to follow the advice of the supplier and the manufacturer carefully.

Silicon sealing

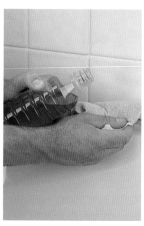

1 To seal between the tiles and the bath, clean the junction of the tiled edge and the tub with some denatured alcohol to remove any surface impurities on the bath's edge. It evaporates quickly to provide a clean surface for the sealant.

2 Apply masking tape along both the bath's edge and the edge of the tiled surface, making sure that the tape is stuck down along the entire length. Leave the joint of the tile–bath junction exposed.

3 Cut off the end of a tube of sealant so that the diameter of the hole will span the joint size created between the two lengths of masking tape. Cut the hole at a slightly diagonal angle – this will allow it to be drawn smoothly along the tile–bath junction.

Porosity

> You can tell that a tile or grout is porous if it darkens when you drop a little water on its surface.

> Penetrating sealers form an invisible barrier that resists moisture and stains. No sealing is absolutely foolproof, however. Any stains or spillages should still be dealt with immediately.

6 While the sealant is still wet, carefully remove the tape to leave a neat siliconed joint. If any area of the joint pulls away as the tape is removed, carefully smooth the sealant back in position with a dampened finger.

4 Fit the tube of sealant into a sealant gun. Applying even pressure on the trigger of the sealant gun, draw the cut end of the tube along the tile–bath junction, between the two strips of masking tape. Create a bead of sealant large enough to just cover the edges of the masking tape strips.

5 With a dampened finger, carefully smooth across the surface of the bead of sealant in one continuous, steady motion.

Alternative seals

Although silicone sealant in a tube is the most commonly used and versatile system for waterproofing a joint, there are other alternatives:

> Sealant dispensers: Silicone sealants in a range of colours to match the most common bathroom suites are available in syringe-like dispensers.

> Quadrant tiles: These can be applied along a tile–fixture junction, using a silicone sealant as the adhesive to fix them in place.

> Plastic sealant strips: These are applied to a tile–fixture junction using double-sided waterproof tape.

> Wooden strips: As long as the wood has had several coats of varnish, decorative wooden mouldings can be used to seal along a junction, using silicone sealant as the adhesive.

floors

Different floorings will require different methods of installation. It's important to understand the surface you are working on and its compatibility with the types of tile you wish to use.

Concrete
This type of subfloor is an excellent surface for tiling, though it may need repairing if it's damaged. Fill small cracks with a mortar mix from a home renovation store followed by a levelling compound, if necessary. Large or deep cracks, particularly if they go right across the room, are best referred to a professional for advice.

Floorboards
Wooden suspended floorboards can't have tiles laid directly on top of them. The floor must first be covered with 15 mm (½ inch) thick exterior grade or marine plywood, which will stand up to the moisture of the adhesive. Some installers prefer a special cement backerboard; these cement and fibreglass panels are attached to the floor with adhesive and screws. The joints between the panels are covered with fibreglass tape.

Vinyl/linoleum
Uncushioned vinyl or linoleum floors can sometimes have tiles laid on top of them if they are well stuck down and the subfloor is in good condition. They just need to be treated with a special primer first. However, they may deteriorate under the new floor, so lifting them is preferable. Some old forms of resilient tiling were manufactured using asbestos. Don't lift these without professional advice.

Existing old tiles or flagstones
Old tiled floors can often be restored, with broken or worn tiles replaced, and in the worst cases, the whole floor lifted and relaid. If you propose to renew the floor completely, consider having it lifted and sold for salvage rather than covering it with floor-levelling compound or a new hard base. Recycle it: your old floor may be just what someone is looking for. Then you'll have more in your budget from the sale of the old floor to put toward the new one.

Underlay options
Waterproof membranes are used in high-moisture areas to prevent water migrating through to the structures under the tiles. Available in sheet form, trowel-on or roll-on liquid, they are essential if you are planning an installation in a wet area.

Crack-isolation membranes help prevent cracks in tiles and grout. They are also available in either sheet form or trowel-on with reinforcing fabric. They are often recommended for use under glass tiles.

Backerboards (CBUs, or cementious backer units) provide a stable, water-resistant underlay for tiles wherever you use them. They come in a variety of sizes and thicknesses. They don't provide structural strength but rather a stable surface for the tiles. Although water-resistant, in showers you will need a waterproof membrane as well.

Problematic surfaces
Some floor surfaces are too flexible and unstable to take tiles successfully. Surfaces not recommended for tiling include:

> Thin interior-grade plywood

> Chipboard

> Particle board

> Tongue and groove boarding

> Cushioned vinyl flooring

> Existing hardwood floors

installing hard floors

The key feature of many hard floors, such as limestone, slate or brick, is that they tend to be very heavy – so it is important to check that the subfloor can take the weight. Laying hard flooring can be more complicated than installing other floors since it is often difficult to cut, and you will almost always have to grout and seal the floor (even if you are using glazed tiles, it is still essential to seal grout lines).

LARGE-FORMAT TILES
The larger the format, the flatter the wall or subfloor needs to be. This is where the experience and skill of a professional tiler can be well worth paying for.

Ground-level subfloors are usually concrete, or wood laid over concrete, and should be able to support the weight of any hard floor. An upper storey may well have suspended wood subfloors, which may not be able to take the load of heavier materials. Upper storeys in blocks of flats, however, may have suspended concrete subfloors, which are much stronger. Always ask your supplier for advice.

Do not install hard tiles directly onto a wood subfloor since movement of the wood may result in cracking. A layer of 15 mm (⅝ inch) marine plywood will provide a stable base for tiles. The joints should be staggered and not in line with the subfloor joints, and the layer can be given added water-proofing using diluted white glue (see page 234).

▼ Ground floors are often solid, but some (over a basement, for example) are suspended floors needing reinforcement.

preparing the site

Before laying your new floor it is essential that you prepare the site properly. This includes removing the existing floor covering and, if necessary, repairing, strengthening and levelling the underlying subfloor.

You may need to install waterproofing, and some floors require a layer of padding or foam underlay. You may also want to lay special underlay, such as acoustic panels, for sound insulation and as a fire-retardant. If the level of your new floor is higher than the old covering, you may have to trim existing doors and casings.

Laying a wood subfloor

Many houses are built with suspended wood subfloors, especially upstairs. Pull up the existing floor covering and check the condition of the boards. If they are loose, sagging or rotten, replace the affected boards with new ones.

Levelling with marine plywood

It is recommended to reinforce floorboards with 15 mm (⅝ inch) sheets of marine plywood to provide a firm and level base for the floor covering. If the floorboards have already been reinforced with plywood, make sure it is thick enough for the flooring you intend to install. You may first need to lift the plywood to examine the floorboards below and sand them level if necessary. Remove any protruding nails or screws, as these could cause lumps in the new flooring. Smooth dents in the plywood with levelling compound (see step 3, opposite), and check that the floor is absolutely level using a spirit level.

If you are buying new plywood to install, get the timber yard to cut it into sheets sized 1.2 x 0.6 m (4 x 2 feet). Use nails or screws that are no longer than the width of the subfloor plus plywood to avoid accidentally drilling into pipes or cables.

▲ A layer of smooth new plywood makes a perfect tiling surface.

I In a bucket, mix water with white glue (one part glue to two parts water). Paint a coat of diluted glue onto the side of the panels that will be laid onto the subfloor. Allow to dry for about 3 hours. This provides an extra coat of waterproofing.

2 Starting from the longest wall, nail or screw sheets onto the floorboards at 15 cm (6 inch) intervals around the edges and 25 cm (10 inch) intervals elsewhere. Butt sheets tightly together and do not align the seams with the floorboard's joints. Cut sheets with a circular saw to fit at the edges, including notches for doorways and other obstructions.

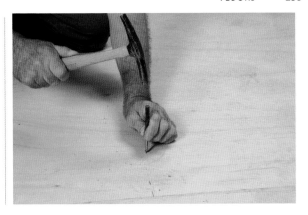

3 Check that the plywood is level using a spirit level and straightedge. Drive protruding nail or screw heads below the surface of the plywood with a nail set. Fill any gaps with levelling compound.

INSTALLING ACOUSTIC PANELS
If you want to install acoustic panels, which offer greater sound insulation than conventional underlay and also provide a particularly level, rigid base for the floor, fix them to the subfloor in the place of plywood. Acoustic panels are thicker than plywood, so check whether you need to trim doors and make any adjustments before laying the floor. Installation systems vary, so ask your supplier for advice and follow the manufacturer's instructions.

techniques for hard floors

Sort hard tiles before laying them out to harmonize variations in tone, size and thickness. Before installation, lay out the whole floor dry to check the overall effect – you might want to alter the position of some tiles if they stand out as being a slightly different colour or shape. It's also essential first to lay out the floor dry when working with any geometric, linear or repeating pattern. Before you start, make a plan of your floor layout on graph paper.

Adhesive or mortar?

Adhesive is simpler to use than mortar as it is supplied ready-mixed, and the precise quantity for the area can be applied straight from the container. Mortar must be mixed with water in a bucket; it sets faster than adhesive and is not recommended for use on a wood subfloor (mortar may rot wood).

Mortar is cheaper than adhesive, however, and if you are confident in handling it, can be quicker to use. It is best used for large, heavy stone tiles and also for brick, when the mortar has to support a large number of bulky items. Adhesive is more convenient for other floors.

Consult your supplier about the recommended bonding material for your particular floor and site.

Spreading the bond

I A plastic spreader is supplied with adhesive; alternatively, buy a 3 mm (⅛ inch) notched trowel for spreading adhesive, and a mason's or brick trowel for mortar. Do not spread more adhesive or mortar than you can use in an hour, or it will set.

2 Push adhesive or mortar over the area with the smooth edge of the spreader or trowel.

3 If you are spreading adhesive, "comb" it with the trowel's notched edge to create furrows. Mortar is not combed, but spread smoothly. Compensate for differences in thickness of tiles by increasing or decreasing the amount of adhesive or mortar used.

Spacing and grouting

Hard tiles are usually spaced and grouted. This is partly to hold them in place, partly to waterproof the floor and partly because natural stone tiles are rarely so regular that their edges would make a perfect fit without gaps. Grouting spaces vary according to the effect desired. The minimum joint is usually about 3 mm (⅛ inch), which creates a precise, contemporary look for modern tiles, such as ceramic. Some floors, such as terracotta, are less exacting in design, and the grouting gaps can be as wide as 2 cm (¾ inch).

Remember that very wide grouting may crack. Sandstone and limestone can be spaced either tightly or loosely, depending on taste and the shape of the tile. Most hard floors need joints of 6 mm–1.25 cm (¼–½ inch). Bricks, however, are often laid butted up without spaces. Always leave at least 3 mm (⅛ inch) for grouting at the edges of the room.

If you have experience in laying floors, you may be able to space tiles by eye, especially when laying heavy tiles that will not move out of place. Otherwise, use spacers to regulate the gaps and keep the tiles from moving while you are laying them out dry. You can buy plastic spacers ranging in width from about 1.5 mm–1.25 cm (¹⁄₁₆–½ inch) or make your own out of bits of wood or even use strips torn from the tile packaging.

Mortar mix

Hard-tile adhesive

THICK THEN THIN

It's easier to use extra adhesive or mortar to bring thin tiles up to the level of thick tiles than the other way around, so lay thicker tiles first, and adjust for the thinner tiles as you go.

cutting hard tiles

Flooring tiles are by their nature thicker than wall tiles and require more powerful equipment to cut them. Don't try to make do with inadequate or flimsy tools, as this will only lead to frustration and possible damage to yourself and others. Organize any power tools you will need in advance, always use gloves and safety glasses, and keep other family members, particularly children, well away from the work area.

Golden rules

> Wear a mask, safety glasses, gloves and ear protection when using power tools.

> Ensure that tiles to be cut are firmly secured in a vise or similar clamp.

It is likely that the tiles you buy will not fit your room exactly, and you will need to cut edge tiles to fit. When using large, expensive tiles, it is worth calculating exactly how much cutting is needed, as remnants can be used to prevent waste. Some hard tiles, such as ceramic or mosaic, can be cut easily using a tile cutter or tile nippers.

Other tiles, such as slate, clay, limestone and sandstone, are harder to cut, and shaping them around corners, pipes and vents requires the use of more powerful tools. Items such as tile cutters, nippers and angle grinders are not expensive to buy, and you can also rent cutting tools from DIY shops, tool rental and tile shops. Use a

straightedge or metal ruler to provide a straight line when scoring or marking tiles for cutting and a try square to mark lines at 90 degrees to the edges. Rough edges can be smoothed with a tile file or sanding block (with coarse-grade sandpaper) or by rubbing the tile with the broken pieces of another tile.

Using the cutting tools

TILE CUTTER
Snap ceramic tiles in half with a tile cutter, which combines a scoring device and lever for snapping. Run the scorer up and down the tile, pressing gently on the lever. Then position the snap mechanism at the top of the scored tile, and press down firmly.

DIAMOND WHEEL CUTTER
If you are cutting many very hard tiles like slate, clay, limestone or sandstone, consider renting a diamond wheel cutter. This is a mechanized tile-cutting saw with a circular blade lubricated by water (change water frequently to prevent clogging). You will still need an angle grinder for curves and corners.

ANGLE GRINDER

An angle grinder fitted with a stone-cutting disk is the best tool to use to cut corners and curves in clay, terracotta, slate, limestone and sandstone tiles. It can also be used for bricks. Work slowly and carefully into your marked outline. Practise on scrap pieces first.

DIAMOND TILE SCORER, COLD CHISEL AND HAMMER

You can snap brick, as well as slate or terracotta tiles (if they are not too thick), with a diamond tile scorer and cold chisel. Score the surface of the tile or brick with a diamond tile scorer and then break it in two with a cold chisel and hammer. Practise on scrap tiles first.

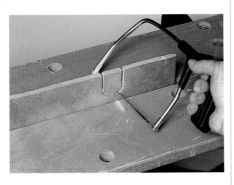

DRILL WITH MASONRY BIT

Use an electric drill with a masonry bit to create tight curves for pipes or curved walls. Drill the area to be removed and then smooth with a half-round file. Also available are hole-cutting drill attachments designed for ceramic tiles, which produce a smooth hole that does not need filing. When fitting, you may have to split the tile in half across the centre of the hole and then lay the halves so that they meet around the pipe.

HAND TILE SAW

Ceramic tiles can also be cut using a hand tile saw, which is essentially a coping or fret saw. This is a useful tool if you have only a few cuts to make, but can be slow to use otherwise. The more expensive type of hand tile saw has a metal frame and is less prone to flexing than saws with a plastic frame. You can also buy tile saw blades to fit your hacksaw.

CUTTING EDGE TILES

A tiled floor should be laid out dry before fixing. Cut edge tiles at this stage. When you reach the edge of the room, place a tile on top of the last whole tile and push it over the empty space until it reaches the wall. Insert spacers between tile and wall to mark what will be the grouting gap. Now mark a cutting line on the bottom tile, adding the extra width of a tile spacer as you draw (to allow for grouting on this side of the tile). Lift out the lower tile and cut along the line to make the edge tile. Alternatively, simply measure the width of the empty space, subtract the width of two grouting gaps and mark a cutting line on the tile. A try square will enable you to draw true lines.

TILE NIPPERS

Tile nippers can be used to cut complicated shapes, such as holes for pipes, from ceramic tiles and to split mosaic tesserae. If you are cutting an L-shape, score the edges of the shape with your tile cutter, but don't snap them. Then use the nippers to remove tile from between the score lines. If you are cutting a curve, mark the curve with a pen, then score a straight line from each end point of the curve and snap this off as usual. Nibble out the remaining part of the curve with the nippers.

Cutting corner tiles

1 Corner cuts are simply straight-edge cuts performed twice on one tile. Make the first cut as for an edge tile (see top left).

2 Then place the cut tile on the floor and position another tile on top to indicate the line for the second cut. Remember to allow for grouting gaps.

MARK IT UP
Before cutting a hard tile, mark the area to be discarded by shading it with a pencil or felt-tipped pen. This will help you avoid cutting too far into the area to be used.

using a template

You can use a cardboard or paper template to help you mark the shape of a pipe, complicated corner or curve on a tile, and then cut out the shape using nippers, a tile saw or an angle grinder.

1 Cut a piece of cardboard to the size of the edge space. Lay the cardboard in place and mark the position of the centre of the pipe.

2 Fold the card on the pipe–centre mark. Then position it with its edge flush to the wall and mark the depth of the pipe from the wall. You now have the outer dimensions of the pipe.

3 Cut the cardboard up the centre mark to the pipe depth, then snip from the side marks to the centre mark, following the shape of the pipe.

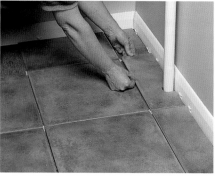

4 Trace around the card template onto the tile, using a pencil (on unglazed tiles) or felt-tipped pen (on glazed tiles). Cut out the shape and fit the tile into position.

grouting

Grout is available in many different colours, ready-mixed or with dye added to a standard mix. Bear in mind that the colour will vary between dry and wet grout – check the finished colour by spreading a small test patch on a scrap piece of wood or cardboard and letting it dry overnight.

1 Don't grout until you are sure that the adhesive or mortar has set properly (leave adhesive overnight and mortar for at least three hours). Use ready-to-mix waterproof, flexible grout. Mix it in a small container, adding water until you achieve a buttery consistency. Work with quantities of about 0.5 L (1 pint) to prevent the grout from drying up in the container (you can increase the quantity as you gain confidence). Stone and brick floors are grouted with mortar mix.

2 Press the grout firmly into the joints using a rubber grouting float – the more compacted the grout is, the harder it will set. Do not allow excess grout to set on the surface of the tiles; wipe it off with a damp cloth or sponge. Wipe only once to avoid pulling grout out of the joints.

3 Pressing down firmly on the grout lines with a small wooden dowel about 1.25 cm (½ inch) in diameter will give an attractive finish and ensure channels for water to run in when the floor is washed. Then polish off any remaining smears of grout with a clean, damp cloth or sponge.

4 If you are laying a floor in a kitchen, bathroom or other wet area, you will need to seal the gaps around the edges of the floor with sealant, applied with a sealant gun. Brick, however, looks better simply grouted at the edges with ready-to-mix mortar.

cutting and laying resilient floors

Resilient floor tiles are thinner and softer than hard floor tiles, meaning that the smallest imperfection in the subfloor will show through. Leather tiling requires expertise to lay well, but other forms of resilient floor tiles, such as cork, vinyl and linoleum, are among the easiest floors to install – a lot easier that the equivalent flooring in sheet form. Sheet is difficult to manœuvre and fit around the edges, whereas you can achieve a smart, professional finish with the equivalent material in tiles. And if your cutting technique needs practice, ruining a couple of tiles in the process is nowhere near as serious as spoiling a whole sheet of flooring material.

How suitable is the subfloor?

Resilient floors are light enough to be laid without problem on suspended wood subfloors. It is, however, essential that the subfloor be smooth and level. Wood floorboards should be levelled with 6 mm (¼ inch) marine plywood and concrete subfloors with levelling compound. If you are laying leather, it is recommended that a wood or concrete subfloor be covered with 2 cm (¾ inch) plywood to ensure a solid base for these expensive tiles. Talk to your supplier about the recommended underlay for your floor.

HEAT TRICK

Heating up a resilient tile with a hair dryer before attempting a complex cut will make the tile more pliable and easier to cut.

Cutting resilient flooring

Unlike hard tiles, which often require powerful cutting tools, resilient flooring can be cut with just a utility knife. Buy a good one, with extra blades. Curved linoleum blades are useful for tougher materials, such as linoleum or rubber, but can be difficult to use with a straightedge. Score with a utility knife and straightedge first, then cut using the linoleum blade.

When you reach the edge of the room, lay a loose tile on top of the last whole tile.

2 Place another tile on top of this and push it over the space between the whole tile and the wall.

3 Mark a cutting line on the middle tile by drawing along the edge of the top tile. Use a try square to draw true lines from your measurements. Cut along the line using a utility knife and straightedge. This will be your edge tile.

TEMPLATES
Make cardboard or paper templates to shape resilient tiles at corners and around obstacles such as bathroom fixtures.

GROUT GAP
If you are laying vinyl with a grout feature strip, remember to allow for the "grout" gap between tiles and around the walls when you are calculating the width of the edge tiles.

CAUTION
Try to avoid cutting tiles on top of already laid tiles as you may damage their surface. Cut tiles on a scrap piece of plywood instead.

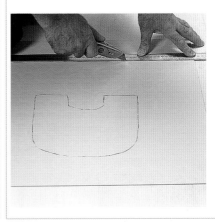

Cleaning

In spite of their tough appearance, it's easy to damage stone and marble surfaces. If you use an inappropriate cleaning product, the damage can be irreversible. Always check the label of your cleaning product and try it out on an inconspicuous area of your tile. If in doubt, don't use it!

Commercial cleaning and polishing machines are excellent for treating large areas of tiles and can be rented by the day. The right cleaning solution, however, is critical.

> Stone and marble

Proper sealing – and maintenance of that sealing – is the best way to maintain stones and marbles and keep them clean. Wipe up spills immediately.

Acid cleaners will remove the polished finish from stones like marble and travertine. Acidic cleaners can also damage grout over a period of time. Use pH-balanced cleaners (there are plenty of specialist suppliers).

Kits can be bought to repair small areas of damage or to repolish small areas of stones or marbles.

To keep an immaculately polished finish, it's probably necessary to bring in the specialists from time to time. These professional refinishers can also help if marble has become badly scratched or damaged.

> Ceramic tiles

Glazed ceramic tiles are easy to clean and maintain. Sweep floors regularly and clean with a recommended tile cleaner (ordinary household cleaners can leave a dirt-attracting residue). For kitchens and bathrooms there are recommended cleaners that will remove limescale, soap and grease residues. These can be brushed on and rinsed away.

> Unglazed ceramic tiles

Terracotta and quarry tiles are generally easy to care for if they have been sealed properly, though they won't resist grease and oil stains as well. Maintaining the sealed surface, and cleaning up regularly, is the best treatment. If the tiles need total refurbishment, then products are available to dissolve old layers of wax, sealer and grease stains, to get the tiles ready for resealing.

> Porcelain tiles

Generally stain resistant, porcelain tiles are easy to care for. It's still advisable to use a sealant to prevent any stain penetration and to use the cleaners recommended by the manufacturers to keep the surface looking good.

> Metal and metallic

Metal tiles are easy to look after. Wash them with a tile cleaner and polish them to a shine. Solid metal tiles can be given a shine with a metal cleaner, but don't use this on metallic ceramic tiles because you'll scratch the finish.

> Glass

Ordinary household glass cleaner will give glass a clean shine.

> Cork

Soft and easily scratched, cork should be swept with a soft brush and mopped using diluted household detergent. Rinse it frequently to avoid making any scratches with grit. Reseal the cork with acrylic varnish when the surface begins to look dull.

> Leather

This needs to be swept gently. Never use water. Clean and buff with wax when needed (not very often). Marks and scratches can't be removed but will just form part of the patina that will develop over time.

> Vinyl and linoleum

These types of floors are easy to clean. Sweep them with a soft broom to remove abrasive particles that might damage the surface, and then wash them with a sponge mop using diluted household detergent. Keep the mop damp rather than sopping wet. Vinyl floor enhancer can be applied every few months to keep up an attractive finish. Vinyl and linoleum floors will need to be stripped back every year or so to prevent excessive build up.

Patches of linoleum hidden from the light (under a rug, for example) may develop a yellowish cast. This will disappear when the linoleum is exposed to light again.

> Rubber

Rubber needs regular cleaning because it tends to mark easily. Solid colours show the dirt quickly. Otherwise, care for rubber as you would for vinyl and linoleum.

sealing floor tiles

Hard tiles are supplied glazed or unglazed. Clay tiles can be either, while ceramic and mosaic are normally glazed. Terracotta, stone and slate tiles are usually unglazed. Unglazed porous tiles must be sealed to prevent stains or spills penetrating the tile surface (slate is naturally waterproof and does not usually need sealing). Sealing is not required for glazed tiles, as nothing can permeate the glaze, but the grout on any floor should be sealed to give it extra waterproofing. This is impractical in the case of mosaic, where there are hundreds of tiny grout lines, so be sure to use a good waterproof grout.

1 Sweep or vacuum the floor before sealing. You can also wipe with a damp, clean cloth to remove dust.

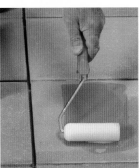

2 Use a paint roller to apply sealant in long strokes and in a consistent direction. Leave overnight to dry (drying times depend on ambient temperature and the porosity of the tiles and grout).

3 If the tiles are glazed, seal only the grout lines, using a 1.25 cm (½ inch) paintbrush. Try not to drop sealant on the tiles and wipe up any spills immediately with a clean cloth.

under-floor heating

When installing a tiled floor, consider installing under-floor heating at the same time. With radiators and floor vents no longer spoiling the style of the room, it frees up a lot of wall and floor space. Under-floor heating gives a pleasant, moderate heat at the lower level of the room, where it's needed (this is particularly good for rooms with high ceilings). It heats the whole space rather than just spot-heating it like other types of heating. The entire floor turns into a gentle radiant heat source. And in family homes, it's good to know that children can't burn themselves on hot radiators or hit themselves on the hard edges.

Under-floor heating is, of course, not new. The Romans heated their tiled floors with warm air carried through ducts beneath the floor. A ducted warm-air system is still available, though many people find it produces too dry an atmosphere in the room. Modern under-floor heating is generally based on either wet systems (like conventional water-radiator systems) or electric systems. Different floorings require different systems, so check with your supplier that the one you have chosen is suitable. Many suppliers have developed their own systems or have ones they recommend.

Wise investments

In any case, good insulation beneath the pipes or cables is crucial. The cheapest form of insulation is expanded polystyrene, but others are available. Electric under-floor heating is cheaper to install than wet pipework (which is quite a fiddly job). Some manufacturers use a system of pipework prelaid into insulated floor panels (which is much quicker). Continuous polyethylene or similar pipework is used, which is durable and has few joints to

leak. Wet systems are most easily installed when you're doing new building work to your home – adding a conservatory or an extension, for example.

Electric under-floor heating is laid as cables or as a textile net where the cable is interwoven or as a very thin foil layer. Single heat mats are available for showers. These accommodate the drain and allow the flooring to dry much more quickly, making it safer sooner. In existing rooms electric under-floor heating is easier to install than a wet system. However, electric under-floor heating is more expensive to run. Budget for it by considering off-peak electricity costs, zone controls and thermostats. Be aware that the more features you have, the more the installation costs. In addition, a system with too many controls will be confusing to understand and operate.

Suitability

Under-floor heating has a slow response rate when heating up or cooling down. It is perhaps a better option for families or the elderly who are home most of the time, rather than for busy folks who come home after

work and need the house to heat up quickly. Because the heat is distributed evenly across the floor area, manufacturers claim that under-floor heating can be more efficient than a conventional radiator or air-vent system, and temperatures can be maintained at two or three degrees lower.

The time it takes to heat up depends on the thickness of the tiles, but once they are heated to a comfortable temperature, there's no difference between thick or thin floor surfaces as far as the level of heat is concerned. Under-floor heating can be installed under both hard and resilient flooring, but make sure you get the right type of heating system for the job.

It is your responsibility to provide suitable electrical wiring and breaken for the installers when installing electric under-floor heating.

▲ Under-floor heating is simpler to install than it used to be, and is a wonderful luxury under bare feet on cold mornings.

resources and suppliers

The tiles pictured in the directory section of this book (pages 54–205) represent types of tile, versions of which should be available from your local tile shop. The following is a list of companies that provided images for the book, and the key below explains the coding system that indicates the page and location of the tiles featured.

KEY:
p = page
r1 = top row (running horizontally)
r2 = second row from top
r3 = third row, etc
r1a) = where row is split, the top tile of the two
r1b) = where row is split, the bottom tile of the two
L = left
M = middle
R = right

American Slate
Tel: 00 1 925 977 4880
Fax: 00 1 800 553 5611
Web: www.americanslate.com
Email: slatexpert@americanslate.com

Black and white: p190 r1R; p191 r2L, r3L

Ann Sacks
Tel: 00 1 800 278 8453
Web: www.annsacks.com

Blue: p154 r2L, r3M
Black and white: p189 r1R, r3L; p191 r1L; p192 r1
Metallics: p201 r2b)R; p205 r2L

Brookforge
Aqua House, Fairfield Street
Leckhampton, Cheltenham
Gloucestershire GL53 0HS
United Kingdom
Tel: 0845 279 9972
Fax: 0845 279 9971
Web: www.brookforge.co.uk
Email: info@brookforge.co.uk

Green: p116 r3R
Black and white: p190 r1M

Capital Marble Design
306 Kensal Road, London
W10 5BE, United Kingdom
Tel: 020 8968 5340
Fax: 020 8968 8827
Web: www.capitalmarble.co.uk
Email: stonegallery@capitalmarble.co.uk

Yellow: p98 r3L

Cork and Floor
Jelinek Cork Group
4500 Witmer Industrial Estates
PMB 167, Niagara Falls
NY 14305-1386
United States
Tel: 00 1 716 439 4644
Fax: 00 1 716 439 4875
Web: www.corkandfloor.com
Email: cork@jelinek.com

Orange: p90 r2R
Neutrals: p177 r3L

Country Floors
Tel: 00 1 800 311 9995
Web: www.countryfloors.com
Email: info@countryfloors.com

Green: p132 r1L, r1R, r2L; p133 r1R
Blue: p154 r1R; p157 r1L
Neutrals: p168 r1a)R; p176 r2; p177 r3R
Black and white: p188 r3R; p192 r2L
Metallics: p205 r1, r2M, r2b)R

CP Group
Armytage Road Industrial Estate
Brighouse
West Yorkshire HD6 1PU
United Kingdom
Tel: 01484 727147
Web: www.cpgroupuk.com
Email: sales@pcgroupuk.com

Red: p79 r1R
Black and white: p189 r1M; p191 r1R

Dalsouple

PO Box 140, Bridgewater
Somerset TA5 1HT
United Kingdom
Tel: 01278 727777
Fax: 01278 727788
Web: www.dalsouple.com
Email: info@dalsouple.com

Red: p62 r1M
Blue: p141 r2M; p143 r1M;
p146 r1M

Dominic Crinson

27 Camden Passage, Islington
London N1 8EA
United Kingdom
Tel: 020 7704 6538
Fax: 0870 046 8199
Web: www.crinson.com
Email: sales@crinson.com

Red: p79 r1L

Edelman Leather

Edelman Leather LLC
80 Pickett Road
New Milford CT 06776
United States
Tel: 00 1 860 350 9600
Fax: 00 1 860 350 3231
Web: www.edelmanleather.com
Email: info@edelmanleather.com

Red: p78 r3L
Orange: p90 r2L, r3a)L

Eluna

GBU LLP Hothouse
London Fields
274 Richmond Road
London E8 3QW
United Kingdom
Tel: 020 7241 7484
Fax: 020 7249 8499
Web: www.eluna.org.uk
Email: info@eluna.org.uk

Green: p132 r3L; p133 r2L
Neutrals: p176 r1M

Fired Earth

3 Twyford Mill, Oxford Road
Adderbury, Nr Banbury
Oxfordshire OX17 3SX
United Kingdom
Tel: 01295 812088
Fax: 01295 810832
Web: www.firedearth.com
Email: enquiries@firedearth.com

Red: p60 r3L; p61 r1L, r1R, r2R;
p62 r2R; p64 r2R; p66 r1L, r1M,
r2L; p67 r1L; p68 r1L; p70 r2L;
p73 r2R; p75 r1R; p78 r2L;
p79 r2L
Orange: p85 r1M; p87 r1, r2, r3;
p88 r3M; p89 r2L
Yellow: p99 r1, r2M; p100 r2R,
r3R; p101 r2M, r3M; p102 r3M;
p103 r2; p104 r1, r2L, r2M, r3R;
p105 r1R, r2R; p106 r1L;
p109 r1R
Green: p114 r3L; p116 r1R;
p117 r2R; p120 r1L, r3L; p121
r2M, r3M; p122 r2L; p123 r1M,
r3L; p127 r1R, r3R; p129 r1L
Blue: p138 r1R, r2L; p139 r1,
r2M; p140 r1, r2R, r3L; p141
r2R, r3M; p142 r1, r2L, r3;
p143 r1L, r1R, r2R; p144 r1L,
r3R; p145 r1M, r2L, r3L; p146
r1L, r1R; p147 r3; p153 r1
Neutrals: p162 r3L; p164 r1L,
r2L; p165 r2M; p167 r1R, r2,
r3L; p168 r2R, r2L; p169 r1;
p171 r1L; p172 r1R; p173 r1L,
r2L; p174 r1L; p177 r2L, r3M
Black and white: p182 r1L, r3M;
p183 r2M, r3R; p184 r2L, r1R;
p185 r3L; p186 r1R, r2R, r3;
p187 r1R, r3; p188 r2R, r3;
p189 r2b)L
Metallics: p198 r1R, r2, r3L;
p199 r1L, r2; p200 r1, r2, r3L;
p201 r1L, r3b)L, r3R; p202 r1M,
r1R, r2; p203 r1L, r1M; p204
r1L, r1R, r2b)M; p205 r2a)R

Globus Cork

741 E-136th Street, Bronx
NY 10454, United States
Tel: 00 1 718 742 7264
Fax: 00 1 718 742 7265

Web: www.globuscork.com
Email: info@corkfloor.com

Red: p79 r3R
Green: p116 r2R
Neutrals: p176 r1R

Haro

Web: www.haro.com

Red: p61 r2L
Orange: p84 r3L
Green: p119 r2L
Blue: p140 r2M
Neutrals: p167 r3M; p169 r3M
Black and white: p184 r1L

Hastings

230 Park Avenue South
New York, NY 10010
United States
Tel: 00 1 212 674 9700
Fax: 00 1 212 674 8083
Web: www.hastingstilebath.com
Email: tile@hastings30.com

Blue: p156 r1R

H&R Johnson

Harewood Street, Tunstall
Stoke-on-Trent ST6 5JZ
United Kingdom
Tel: 01782 524040
Web: www.johnson-tiles.com
Email: factoryoutlet@johnson-
tiles.com

Red: p61 r2M; p62 r1R; p63
r2R; p64 r2L; p65 r3L; p66 r1R,
r2R, r3R
Yellow: p104 r2R; p107 r3
Green: p114 r1L, r2L, r2R, r3M,
r3R; p116 r1L, r1M; p117 r2L;
p118 r1; p119 r1L, r3; p120
r3M, r3R; p123 r1R, r2L, r2R;
p124 r1
Blue: p138 r2M, r3; p139 r2L;
p140 r2L; p141 r3L; p143 r2L;
p144 r2R; p145 r1R, r2R, r3R;
p146 r3R; p149 r1; p152 r3M
Black and white: p188 r1L

Neutrals: p162 r1L, r1M, r2, r3M, r3R; p163 r1L, r2L, r3L, r3R; p164 r1R; p165 r1M, r3L, r3R; p171 r2L
Metallics: p198 r1L, r1M, r3R; p201 r2a)L; p204 r2L

Karndean
Karndean International LLC
Bushy Run Corporate Park
1100 Pontiac Court, Export
PA 15632, United States
Tel: 00 1 724 387 2056
Fax: 00 1 724 387 2057
Web: www.karndean.com
Email: info@karndean.com

Orange: p92 r2R; p93 r3L
Neutrals: p172 r2R; p174 r2L; p175 r2L
Black and white: p183 r3a)L; p186 r1L

Kirkstone
Brigend, Fyvie, Aberdeenshire
AB53 8QB, United Kingdom
Tel: 01651 891891
Fax: 01651 891764
Web: www.kirknaturalstone.com
Email: info@kirknaturalstone.com

Neutrals: p170 r2M; p173 r1M, r1R; p174 r1M
Black and white: p192 r3R

Leafcutter Design
119 Penn Hill Avenue
Lower Parkstone, Poole
Dorset BH14 9LY
United Kingdom
Tel: 01202 716969
Fax: 01202 716969
Web: www.leafcutterdesign.co.uk
Email: sales@leafcutterdesign.co.uk

Red: p78 r1M, r2R
Orange: p91 r3M
Yellow: p109 r2L, r3a)R
Black and white: p190 r2R, r3M; p191 r2R, r3R

Metallics: p204 r2a)M

Marmoleum
Forbo Nairn Ltd, PO Box 1
Kirkcaldy, Fife KY1 2SB
United Kingdom
Tel: 01592 643777
Fax: 01592 643999
Web: www.forbo-flooring.co.uk
Email: info.uk@forbo.com

Red: p67 r1R, r2
Orange: p86 r1L, r1M, r2
Yellow: p105 r1L, r2L, r3L
Green: p117 r2M; p119 r1M, r1R, r2R
Blue: p143 r2M, r3
Neutrals: p162 r1R; p165 r1L; p175 r2R
Black and white: p182 r1R; p188 r2R, r3L

Medici Mosaics
Baskent O.S.B. 205 A. 7.p.06990
Temelli-Ankara, Turkey
Tel: 00 90 312 640 1211
Fax: 00 90 312 640 1292
Web: www.medicimosaics.com
Email: joseph@medicimosaics.com

Red: p61 r3M; p64 r1
Orange: p84 r1M, r3M; p86 r3
Green: p115 r2; p121 r2L

Minton Hollins
Harewood Street, Tunstall
Stoke-on-Trent ST6 5JZ
United Kingdom
Tel: 01782 575575
Fax: 01782 577377
Web: www.johnson-tiles.com
Email: info.uk@forbo.com

Red: p60 r2L; p63 r3L; p73 r3L; p74 r1R; p75 r1L, r1M, r2; p76 r1L, r1b)M, r3M, r3R; p77 r1b)M, r2M
Orange: p89 r1R, r3M; p91 r1, r3R; p92 r1L, r1Mb), r3M, r3R; p93 r1

Yellow: p98 r1R; p99 r2R; p101 r2L; p102 r1R, r2M; p103 r1; p104 r3M
Green: p115 r1R; p125 r3L; p129 r1a)R, r3L; p130 r1L, r1M, r2c)R; p131
Blue: p141 r2L; p145 r2M, r3M; p148 r3R; p149 r2M; p150 r1a)L, r1b)L, r1R; p152 r1
Neutrals: p168 r1b)M; p175 r3L
Black and white: p182 r2R; p183 r2L; p189 r2b)L

Original Style
Falcon Road
Sowton Industrial Estate, Exeter
Devon EX2 7LF, United Kingdom
Tel: 01392 473001
Fax: 01392 473003
Web: www.originalstyle.com
Email: info@originalstyle.com

Red: p61 r1M; p63 r1R; p64 r2M, r3L; p68 r1R, r2b)R, r3R; p69; p70 r1M, r1R, r2R, r3a)R; p71 r2L; p72; p73 r1R; p74 r1L, r1M, r2L; p76 r2M, r2R; p77 r1L, r1a)M, r1R, r3a)M, r3b)M, r3R
Orange: p85 r1L, r2L, r3L; p89 r1L, r1M, r2M, r3L; p92 r1Ma), r1R, r3L
Yellow: p98 r1L; p100 r2L, r2M; p101 r1R; p102 r2R; p104 r3L; p106 r1R, r2; p107 r1, r2; p108; p109 r1L
Green: p114 r1R; p115 r1L; p120 r1R; p123 r1L; p124 r2L, r2R; p125 r1, r2; p126 r2R; p127 r1a)L, r1b)L, r2L, r2M; p128 r1a)R, r1b)R, r2; p129 r2; p130 r1R, r2a)R, r2b)R, r3R
Blue: p138 r1L, r1R, r2R; p139 r2R; p140 r3R; p141 r1, r3R; p142 r2M; p144 r1R; p145 r1L; p146 r1b)R, r2R, r3L; p147 r1L; p148 r1, r2; p149 r2R; p150 r3a)R, r3b)R; p151 r1L, r1R, r3R; p152 r2L, r2a)M, r2b)M, r2R; p153 r2L
Neutrals: p163 r3M; p164 r2R, r3R; p165 r1R, r2L, r2R; p167 r1L, r3R; p168 r3R; p169 r2L;

p170 r1, r3R; p172 r1b)M, r2L, r3L; p173 r3L; p174 r1R, r2R, r3R; p175 r1; p177 r1, r2R
Black and white: p182 r3L; p184 r1M; p185 r1M; p186 r2M; p187 r1L, r2L; p188 r3M; p189 r1a)L, r1b)L, r2M; p193
Metallics: p201 r1a)R; p202 r1L; p203 r1R, r2

RAK Ceramics
Paris House, Frenchmans Road
Petersfield, Hampshire
GU32 3JB United Kingdom
Tel: 01730 815507
Fax: 01730 267933
Web: www.rakceramics.co.uk
Email: info@rakceramics.co.uk

Red: p62 r1L
Green: p129 r1b)R
Neutrals: p166; p168 r1L; p170 r2L; p171 r2R
Black and white: p183 r1L
Metallics: p201 r3R

Royce Wood Studio
The Wheelhouse, Amber Mill
Toadhole Furnace, Oakerthorpe
Alfreton, Derbyshire DE55 7LL
United Kingdom
Tel: 01773 835411
Fax: 01773 835411
Web: www.roycewood.com
Email: sales@roycewood.co.uk

Orange: p90 r3M; p91 r3L
Yellow: p109 r3M
Metallics: p204 r2a)R, r2b)R

Rupert Scott
The Glass Studio
Rhodiad-Y-Brenin, St Davids
Wales SA62 6PJ, United Kingdom
Tel: 0845 450 7684
Fax: 0845 017 7685
Web: www.rupertscott.com
Email: glass@rupertscott.com

Red: p78 r1L, r1R, r3R
Yellow: p109 r3b)R

Green: p116 r2L, r3M; p133 r3L, r3R
Neutrals: p176 r1L
Black and white: p190 r2a)M
Metallics: p204

Sicis
470 Broome Street, New York
NY 10013, United States
Tel: 00 1 212 965 4100
Fax: 00 1 212 343 7036
Web: www.sicis.com
Email: info@sicis.com

Red: p64 r3R; p65 r1, r2
Orange: p86 r1R
Green: p117 r1; p118 r2; p120 r2R; p121 r1R, r3L; p122 r1
Blue: p145 r3R; p151 r3M
Neutrals: p163 r1R; p171 r1R; p172 r1L; p173 r2L
Black and white: p183 r1R; p185 r2L

Stone Age Limited
Unit 3, Parsons Green Depot
Parsons Green Lane, London
SW6 4HH, United Kingdom
Tel: 020 7384 9090
Fax: 020 7384 9099
Web: www.estone.co.uk
Email: enquiries@estone.co.uk

Orange: p90 r3R
Black and white: p192 r2a)R

Stone Source
215 Park Avenue South
New York, NY 10003
United States
Tel: 00 1 212 979 6400
Fax: 00 1 212 979 6989
Web: www.stonesource.com
Email: info@stonesource.com

Orange: p90 r1R
Yellow: p109 r3L
Green: p116 r2M, r3L; p133 r1L
Black and white: p190 r1L, r2b)M

Walls and Floors
Wilson Terrace, Kettering
Northamptonshire NN16 9RT
United Kingdom
Tel: 01536 314730
Fax: 01536 410711
Web: www.wallsandfloors.co.uk
Email: info.uk@forbo.com

Orange: p90 r1L
Green: p124 r2M
Black and white: p191 r3M

Winchester Tiles
Falcon Road, Exeter
Devon EX2 7LF
United Kingdom
Tel: 01392 473001
Fax: 01392 473003
Web: www.winchestertiles.com
Email: info@winchestertiles.com

Red: p60 r1; p61 r3R; p62 r3L; p68 r2a)R; p70 r1L, r3R; p71 r1, r3; p73 r1L; p76 r1M; p79 r2R
Orange: p84 r1L, r1R, r2; p88 r3L; p90 r1M, r2M, r3b)L
Yellow: p98 r1M, r2, r3R; p99 r2L; p100 r1, r3L; p101 r1L, r3L; p102 r1L, r3L, r3R; p109 r2R
Green: p114 r2M; p115 r1M; p121 r1L, r1M, r3R; p125 r3R; p128 r1L
Blue: p146 r2M, r3M; p149 r2L; p150 r1M, r2L, r2M, r3M; p151 r1M, r2L, r3L; p153 r3R
Neutrals: p171 r3L
Black and white: p183 r1M; p185 r1L

World's End Tiles
Silverthorne Road, Battersea
London SW8 3HE
United Kingdom
Tel: 020 7819 2100
Fax: 020 7819 2101
Web: www.worldsendtiles.co.uk
Email: info@worldsendtiles.co.uk

Black and white: p190 r2L

Index

A

accent tiles 30
acoustic panels 235
adhesives 208–209, 218–219, 236
all-over tiling 22
angle grinder 239
antique tiles 48–49

B

basket-weave pattern 12
bathrooms 21–22
black and white tiles 179–193
blue tiles 135–157
border tiles 30
borders 17
boxing in 214–215
brick-bond pattern 10
budgets 15, 41, 207

C

ceramic tiles 28–31
choosing tiles 13, 14
cleaning
    antique tiles 49
    resilient tile floors 246–247
cold chisel 239
colour 13, 29
    of grout 208, 243
    see also black and white tiles;
        blue tiles; green tiles; metallic
        tiles; neutral colours; orange
        tiles; red tiles; yellow tiles
complementary colours 58, 66,
    82, 96, 112, 136
concrete floors 232
cork tiles 50–51
corners
    applying adhesive 218
    boxing in 215
    cutting tiles for 241
    tiling 225–227
costs 15, 41, 207
cutting
    curves 215
    tiles 222–224, 244–245
    trimming doors 212
cutting tools 211, 215, 222, 224,
    238–239, 240

D

delft tiles 31
designs, for flooring 10–12,
    16–17, 236
diamond tile scorer 239
diamond wheel cutter 238
digitally printed tiles 46
dining rooms 19–20
doors, trimming 212
drill with masonry bit 239
drilling, porcelain tiles 222

E

ear protectors 211
edges 15
    cutting edge tiles 240
    and "grout gap" 245
    stone tiles 39
electric
    tools 239
    under-floor heating 248
elevations 16
encaustic tiles 31
entranceways 23
environment 9, 51, 67
epoxy grout 20, 209
estimating the number of tiles 212
ethical sourcing 41
external corners 227

F

facemasks 211
fake stone tiles 34–35
field tiles 30
finishes 15
    ceramic tiles 28
    stone tiles 38, 39
floor levels 15
floorboards 232
flooring
    cutting tiles for 222
    designs for 10, 11, 12
    Roman 170
    tiles for 31, 43
    tiling techniques 207
    types of 12, 232
    see also hard tile floors; resilient
        tile floors

G

geometric floor tiles 31
glass tiles 42–43
    cutting 222
    and metals 203
glasses, safety 211, 222
glazed tiles 28, 247
gloves, protective 211
grey tiles 180
green tiles 111–133
grout 20, 47, 208–209
    applying 228–229, 237, 243
    sealing 247
"grout gap" 245

H

halls 23, 72
hammer 239
hand tile saw 239
hard tile floors 12, 233–243
    cutting 238–242
    grouting 243, 247
    installing 233
    preparation of 234–235
    sealing 247
    techniques for 236–237
heat trick, for resilient tiles 244
heating, under-floor 15, 248–249
herringbone pattern 10
holes, drilling 222

I

insert tiles, metal 200, 202, 203
insulation, and heating 248
internal corners 225–226

J

jigsaw 215

K

kitchens 19–20

L

large-format tiles 15, 233
layouts, for flooring 10–12,
    16–17, 236
leather tiles 50, 51

level
of floors 15
of starting point 216–217
of tiles 226, 237
lighting, for glass tiles 42
limestone 38
linoleum floors 232
linoleum tiles 52
living rooms 24
lustre tiles 30

M

machine cutting 224
marble 38
marine plywood 234–235
marking up 241, 242, 245
matching up 16
measuring 216–217, 223, 226
mesh- or paper-backed tiles 30
metallic tiles 44–45, 195–205, 222
mouldings 31
mortar 209, 236
mosaic tiles 46–47

N

neutral colours 159–177

O

octagon patterns 12
old tiles, tiling over 213, 232
orange tiles 81–93
ordering (buying) tiles 212
outdoor areas 25

P

panels, acoustic 235
paper- or mesh-backed tiles 30
patterns, of tiles 10–12
pebble floors 40
picture tiles 46–47
pinwheel pattern 12
plastic quadrants 227
plastic sealant strips 231
plywood 234–235
pool tiles 25
porcelain tiles 34–35
adhesives for 209
cutting and drilling 222
porosity 230, 247

Q

quadrant tiles 231
quadrants, plastic 227
quarry tiles 33

R

recycled glass 43
red tiles 57–79
resilient tile floors 12
cleaning 246–247
cutting and laying 244–245
sealing 247
Roman floor 170
rubber gloves 211
rubber tiles 52, 53
running board pattern 12

S

safety equipment 211, 213, 222, 238
safety glasses 211, 222
Saltillo tiles 33
salvage yards 49
sandstone 38
scale plans 16
sculpted tiles 30
sealant dispensers 231
sealing
floor tiles 243, 247
wall tiles 230–231
silicon sealing 230–231
sizes
combining different 17, 140, 190
small-format tiles 15, 18
slate 39
small-format tiles 15, 18
smalti tiles 42
spacing/spacers 208, 226, 237, 245
square with inserts pattern 10
stone tiles 36–41
subfloors 233, 234–235, 244
sunken bath 33
surfaces, unsuitable for tiling 232
see also finishes; glazed tiles

T

templates 242, 245
terracotta tiles 32
textures, contrast of 19, 35
thresholds 212
tile cutters 222, 224, 238
tile nippers 240
tile pavement pattern 10
tiling gauge 216–217
tools 210–211
for adhesives 218, 219, 236
for cutting 211, 215, 222, 224, 238–239, 240
for measuring 216–217, 223
transfer-print tiles 30
travertine 38
tube lining 30

U

under-floor heating 15, 248–249
underlays 232, 234

V

vinyl floors 232
vinyl tiles 52, 53

W

walls 213–231
applying adhesives 218–219
applying first tiles 220–221
boxing in 214–215
corners 225–227
cutting tiles for 222–224, 226
grouting and polishing 228–229
preparation of 213
sealing the tiles 230–231
starting level 216–217
tiling techniques 207
wastage 16
white and black tiles 179–193
wooden
strips 231
subfloors 234–235
work gloves 211

Y

yellow tiles 95–109

Credits

Quarto would like to thank and acknowledge the following for supplying the illustrations and photographs reproduced in this book.

Key: a above, b below, l left, r right

p1 Royce Wood
p2, p3, p27, p30ar, p39r, p249 Fired Earth
p4, p22, p30br, p34, p42 Surface Tiles
(Tel: 020 7819 2300 www.surfacetiles.com)
p8, p17a, p20b, p23, p24b, p30bc, p30tc, p31b, p40a, p211 Original Style
p13a, p43, p96 Douglas Hill/Beateworks/Corbis
p13b Andy Crawford/Gettyimages
p14 American Slate Company
p15, p33bl, p45, p47b, p59, p113, p136 Tim Street-Porter/Beateworks/Corbis
p16 The CP Group
p17b Pilkingtons
p18, p20a Porcelanosa (Tel: 0800 915 4000 www.porcelanosa.co.uk)
p19, p28, p30c, p44 Ann Sacks
p21 CP Group
p23al, p32, p36, p38bl,br, p46 Paris Ceramics
p24a Karndean International
p25 Marston & Langinger (Tel: 0845 270 6688 www.marston-and-langinger.com)
p29 Roger Brooks/Beateworks/Corbis
p30cr, p33cr Robert O'Dea/Red Cover/Gettyimages
p30al Minton Hollins
p30bl, p31ar Winchester Tiles
p31ac,ar London Mosaics
p35a Fernando Bengoechea/Beateworks/Corbis
p35b NicholasKane/Arcaid/Corbis
p37, p54 Scott Van Dyke/Beateworks/Corbis
p39l Kirk Natural Stone
p41br, p160 Dana Hoff/Beateworks/Corbis
p41bl Michel Arnaud/Beateworks/Corbis
p41ar Richard Ross/Corbis
p47a Elliott Kaufman/Beateworks/Corbis
p48 V&A Images
p49 The Bridgeman Art Library/Gettyimages
p50 Edelman Leather Very Natural Floor Tiles

p51 Dualoy Leather
p52 Litwin Photography/Shutterstock
p55 Rob Melnychuk/Taxi/Gettyimages
p58, p197 Johnny Bouchier/Red Cover/Gettyimages
p40b, p82, p112 Abode/Beateworks/Corbis
p83 Ron Chapple Stock/Corbis
p97, p196 Red Cover/Gettyimages
p137 Pieter Estersohn/Beateworks/Corbis
p161 David Papazian/Corbis
p180 Sara Zinelli/Red Cover/Gettyimages
p181 Neil Lorimer/Elizabeth Whiting & Associates/Corbis
p206 Madeleine Openshaw/Shutterstock
p233 Jon Bouchier/EWA Stock

The images featured in the directory section of this book are credited in Resources and Suppliers, pages 250–253.

All other illustrations and photographs are the copyright of Quarto Publishing plc. Whilst every effort has been made to credit contributors, Quarto would like to apologize should there have been any omissions or errors – and would be pleased to make the appropriate correction for future editions of the book.